Major Contributors to Social Science Series

ALFRED MC CLUNG LEE, General Editor

Lester Frank Ward

ISRAEL GERVER

The American University, Washington, D.C.

THOMAS Y. CROWELL COMPANY

New York, Established 1834

Editor's Foreword

Undergraduates often find a great challenge in reading a seminal thinker's major contributions to social science in their original form. But students are usually offered either volume-length works containing stimulating passages embedded in outworn discussions, or brief excerpts included with those of other authors in general collections of readings. The longer works tend to be repetitious and wordy, and some now appear misguided. At the same time, excerpts in general collections do not give enough of a contributor's work to make him come alive.

In planning the present series, John T. Hawes, Director of the College Department of the Thomas Y. Crowell Company, and I sought manuscripts free from either of the above weaknesses. The editors were asked to dig out the main lines of a contributor's method and thought from the verbiage and the dated materials obscuring them, and to make available, in one slim volume, a critical essay together with the most significant and interesting passages in a contributor's writings. The volumes in the series, considered as a whole, thus give the student an understanding of the diverse ways of thought that have gone into the making of the social science discipline as we now know it.

The series has been edited and written so that each little book can be read for its own merits and without need of additional props. Each contains the seminal ideas of an author which still remain alive today but does not gloss over his weaknesses. Each book provides a critical vignette of the social scientist as he is now seen. Each book, too, should be interesting to college sophomores and especially to undergraduate majors in the various social sciences.

What all volumes in the series have in common is an educative conception. They are all efforts to interest undergraduates in some of the great "originals" of social science and thus to stimulate further exploration of important ideas and methods. The editor-critic who has done each volume has been free to follow his own professional judgment in analyzing his major contributor and in selecting significant excerpts from his works. Each volume thus has an individuality deriving from its editor-critic as well as from its subject.

The books in this series are intended to enrich introductory courses in the various social sciences. For more advanced courses, they will permit the student to become acquainted with the meatiest contributions of many selected social scientists rather than the few whose works he might read more extensively. Advanced students will find these books invaluable for the purposes of review.

ALFRED MC CLUNG LEE

Preface

This volume of selections from the extensive corpus of sociological writings of Lester Frank Ward is offered as an example of the work of a rare order of intellect who also happened to be one of the founders of the discipline of sociology. While fashions in sociological thought and modes of analysis have changed since Ward's day, his concerns with the enduring features of social life are quite similar to the substantive interests of sociologists in our time. The mysteries of the market economy, for example, are always with us, as are the enigma of the social role of women and the puzzling phenomena of intellectual, scientific, and artistic creativity, social and intrapersonal conflict, and social planning.

At the moment this is the only selection of Ward's writings in print, and I have selected the specific items with one major end in view: the relevancy of the topic and of Ward's analysis to the sociologist who is engaged with similar topics today. I have leaned heavily on four treatises, listed below as the sources of excerpts for this collection. These constitute Ward's major works in the field, and they pose a problem for the anthologist in that they are not easily susceptible to reduction and condensation. As a result, I have selected large portions of sections which represent Ward somewhat shorn of the nineteenth-century academic garb of systematic large-scale theory and coined terminology that he indulged in.

I have not attempted to present him as a systematic philosopher of history. Rather, I have chosen to present him as a sociological commentator on various issues. The Contents indicates the scope of his curiosity and the versatility of his sociological interests.

For the general reader, this anthology provides a glimpse into the mind of a unique American scientist. For the student of sociological theory, it offers examples of sociological analysis that still retain pertinency and saliency after more than half a century. In addition, this volume, together with the others in this series, gives the student an understanding of the diverse ways in which eminent sociologists have analyzed their scientific problems.

Following are the full titles of those of Ward's writings that are the sources of the excerpts in this volume:

Dynamic Sociology (New York: D. Appleton and Company, 1883, 1910), 2 vols.

The Psychic Factors of Civilization (Boston: Ginn and Company, 1893, 1906).

Pure Sociology: A Treatise on the Origin and Spontaneous Development of Society (New York: The Macmillan Company, 1903).

Applied Sociology: A Treatise on the Conscious Improvement of Society by Society (Boston: Ginn and Company, 1906).

I would like to acknowledge the help of several colleagues, notably Alfred McClung Lee, George Simpson, and Richard Mendes, all of Brooklyn College, who in discussions encouraged me to explore the work of Lester Ward. I would especially like to thank Miss Carla Drige for her invaluable typing. Finally, with gratitude and affection, I dedicate this volume to my wife Joan and our children, Joseph, Michael, and Jane.

I. G.

New York City
January, 1963

Contents

Editor's Foreword   v

Preface   vii

Introduction   1

1. The Person and Society   6

    Happiness   6
    Feeling, Function, and Action   8
    Social Action   10
    Social Friction   12
    Economy of Nature and Mind   23
    The Social Intellect   26

2. Social Patterns of Behavior   31

    General Characteristics of Pure Sociology   31
    Subject-Matter of Sociology   32
    Methodology   34
    Biologic Origins of the Subjective Faculties   35
    The Phylogenetic Forces   36
    Biological Origins of Objective Faculties   54

3. The Consequences of Social Action   58

Relation of Pure to Applied Sociology   58
The Efficacy of Effort   60
End or Purpose of Sociology   63
Truth and Error   72
Social Appropriations of Truth   85

Lester Frank Ward

Introduction

Lester Frank Ward (1841–1913) was the youngest of ten children born to Justus and Silence (Rolph) Ward. Justus Ward has been described by his son's principal biographer, Samuel Chugerman,* as an itinerant mechanic who sought to make a paradise for his family in the American West by homesteading and other ventures, all unprofitable. The family was poor, but the diary of the young Lester Frank Ward shows that his boyhood was not so burdened by extreme hardship as has often been assumed.† His father died when Ward was sixteen, and he was on his own from then on.

The young Ward earned a meager livelihood by working on farms and in mills. However, he had a passion for educating himself. He taught himself Greek and French, and pursued an interest in biology and botany which he had acquired during hunting expeditions on the prairies. Thus he laid a groundwork, if an unsystematic one, for his later scientific investigations. Ward literally educated himself. In 1861, at the age of 20, he entered a preparatory school, but this was a luxury that he could afford for only a single semester.

In August, 1862, he enlisted in the Union Army, and served 27 months. In 1864 he was wounded. After his discharge late in that year, while he was still recuperating from his wounds, he entered Government civil service in Washington, D.C., and by the next year he had attained a post as a clerk in the Treasury. In 1867, at the age of 26, Ward moved to the Bureau of Statistics, and at this time he enrolled for college work. His college entrance examinations brought such high grades that in spite of the fact that he was not a qualified

---

* Samuel Chugerman, *Lester F. Ward: The American Aristotle* (Durham, N.C.: Duke University Press, 1939).

† See B. J. Stern, ed., *Young Ward's Diary* (New York: G. P. Putnam's Sons, 1935.)

1

student in the formal sense, Columbia University in Washington, D.C., not only admitted him to a new evening program, thus allowing him to continue to earn his living during the day, but granted him sophomore standing. He was awarded the B.A. in 1870 and the M.A. in 1872. In 1871 he had also won diplomas in law and medicine at Johns Hopkins.

Ward now directed his great intellectual energies toward writing and research. After a series of responsible positions in various governmental departments, in 1883 he became chief paleontologist of the U.S. Geological Survey. He had also started to write the first of his sociological treatises, Dynamic Sociology; when it appeared in 1883 it irritated Spencerians but drew no appreciable response from other social scientists or from the general public. None the less, the book established Ward as a great pioneer of modern and evolutionary sociology in the United States. Dynamic Sociology was followed by The Psychic Factors of Civilization (1893), and Outlines of Sociology (1898). Two later works, Pure Sociology (1903), and Applied Sociology (1906), recapitulate Ward's overall thought. The Textbook of Sociology (1905), by Ward and J. Q. Dealey, is in large part an abridgment of Pure Sociology. Ward did not have a full-time position with a university until 1906, when he joined the staff of Brown. He died in 1913, having attained an amazing record of accomplishment in his 72 years of life.

Today, none of his work is in print. His efforts are comparable to those of an old master whose work is kept in storage and never exhibited. This is partly accountable to the tendency of most American sociologists to ignore historical antecedents and to value only those earlier ideas and accomplishments that have an obvious and direct relation to the present. Yet in leaving Ward in eclipse, sociologists are making a mistake, and their willingness to remain blind to his merits is not easily explained.

Early in his introduction to that curious and cumbersome tome, The Structure of Social Action, Talcott Parsons reiterated Crane Brinton's query, "Who now reads Spencer?" Parsons suggested that Spencer's archaic social theory accounted for his failure to survive as an intellectual force today. Parsons justified the neglect of that overly ambitious cosmologist on the grounds that the positivistic-utilitarian tradition which he so eminently represented was essentially sterile and lacking in present-day relevance.

Parsons could have gone on to ask: "Who now reads any of the founding fathers of sociological theory," since Comte, Ward, and, to a lesser extent, Marx, are also regarded as unworthy of more than antiquarian interest. Robert Merton summarily evaluated the early sociologists as highly talented men who, in the final analysis, made few meaningful contributions to the issues with which sociologists are concerned today.

However, while one can convict these nineteenth-century theorists of having committed grievous errors as measured by our own canons of logical rigor—for instance, a lack of genuine correspondence between their empirical evidence and their conceptual frame of reference—one cannot deny their significance as pioneers. This alone would not be enough to insure remembrance; but in addition these men made substantive contributions which transcend their methodological inadequacies, as any reading of their work will demonstrate. Why, then, are they neglected? Why are Lester Frank Ward's works largely unread and long out of print?

Several probable explanations emerge. One of these is that since sociology has modeled itself upon the image of the physical sciences, it can no longer strive, as in the days of the pioneers, to serve also as a philosophy of history, or to interpret phenomena in terms of a world view. Sociologists are more and more preoccupied with problems of theoretical formulation, methodological assumptions, and conceptual precision—all geared toward the pursuit of empirical research and thereby solidifying the image of sociology as a respectable scientific endeavor.

A second possible explanation is that each new generation tends to redefine ideas in terms and emphases that are relevant to contemporary concerns and thereby to disregard older formulations. This not only promotes the idea that sociology is a growing science, but also lends an air of originality to ideas which are actually old. Ignorance of the past is indispensable for this form of sociology. The modern sociologists like to feel that as the discipline moves in the direction of research and verification and of specific hypotheses characteristic of a "real" science, the older ideas are not only discarded, but are dumped in the intellectual garbage heap.

There is a cleavage among sociologists, and the oddest aspect of this is that two types of illiteracy exist. The younger, "scientifically" oriented, know little and care less about their intellectual ancestors, while their older colleagues view the past with nostalgia and reverence, and at times uphold it uncritically, crying out that the original discipline has been sold out in favor of a false image of the rewards of science. This latter is a form of illiteracy in that the older sociologists often fail to deal with newer propositions on their own terms, but attack them as unoriginal, as if any concept could be truly original. Naturally, I am describing the extremes here, since most sociologists have been torn between these two divergent influences. As is usual with extreme positions, both are wrong. The younger sociologists fail to realize that their positions were set forth by Ward and like-minded men over fifty years ago. The older orientation would adhere too literally to an outmoded system.

It is a fact that Ward's formal system is based on four postulates which are totally inacceptable today. There are (1) Spencerian evolution, which Ward adopted and used as a basis for a lifelong polemic against Spencer and his disciples; (2) its bifurcated stepchildren genesis and telesis; (3) that vaguest of notions, the concept of social forces; and (4) the Hegelian construct, the principle of synergy. These postulates can easily be attacked and discarded. Timasheff has noted that as conceptual tools they account for the diffuseness and inconsistencies of Ward's treatises. The anti-Spencer polemic, while damaging in its time, is today a tiresome tirade which obscures Ward's own brilliant insights and incisive observations.

Nonetheless, it is important that we should not lose sight of Ward. The portions of his work that are most significant are those that reveal him as stimulated by his keen observations of the world about him. His formal conceptual scheme may intrude on occasion, but his chief concern is always with the substantive issue, and, more largely, with men's problems and endeavors and achievements. Scholarship for Ward was purely a device for amplifying and deepening the significance of his observations. There is a provocative element of the personal in his writing, an invitation to the reader to share in his enthusiasms and despairs, and to be persuaded of his evaluations.

What is often ignored in assessing Ward is the fact that he is the only genuine physical scientist among all the older sociologists. He was a respected and recognized paleontologist and a practicing geologist. One finds in his geological papers and researches a meticulous coverage of prior literature and a careful examination of the empirical data, as well as evaluations of his colleagues' works which are uniquely helpful to us today as we form our own estimation of those works. In particular, Ward made one contribution towards a prominent mode in present-day sociological theory, the structural functional theory.*

* See for example, Talcott Parsons, The Social System (New York: The Free Press of Glencoe, Inc., 1951).

His training in geology, biology, stratigraphy, and paleobotany, was responsible for this approach. The analogical thought models and especially the structural concepts in those sciences are similar to those of sociology.

We should also realize that Ward grasped issues that have in no way lost their importance for us today, such as the role of women, the legislative process, the role of deception and the ruse in social affairs and especially in political life, the social consequences of professionalization, crime and deviancy, romantic and conjugal love, and social welfare.

Ward was a presager of Durkheimian sociology, especially in his analysis of religion and other institutions. He has never received his rightful due as a major link in the chain that leads to contemporary theory, especially the Durkheimian variety.

Ward's work is shot through with a passionate concern for social reform and the promotion of a liberal ideology. His insights and perceptions reveal him as the epitome of the concerned human being who uses his learning in order to comprehend and help the world about him. He is characteristically the opposite of the European savants who see nothing ahead but doom. Ward sees human beings purposively shaping their own destinies through a perfection of social mechanisms and institutions. While he is a child of the Enlightenment, he is not a Pollyanna. He recognizes evils and follies, but insists upon reasoning problems through before acting upon them, since he belongs among the sociological analysts and not among sentimental social reformers or blind activists.

Unlike his archenemy Spencer, whose cosmological evolutionary approach he adopted, Ward does not see social evolution as automatic and inevitable. Progress, rather, is achieved by intellect and reason. Meliorism rather than laissez-faire is the order of the day. Also, unlike Comte, Ward was not interested in imposing an authoritarian order upon society, but rather in the goal-directed action of individual men and women.

The neglect of Ward, and of intellectual ancestors generally, reflects the narrow interests of many professional sociologists. But the fact remains that the ideas of the nineteenth century have helped to shape those of the twentieth. Indeed, the realization that the history of ideas is not of antiquarian interest alone may restrain ahistorical sociologists from promoting unwittingly old ideas under the guise of new ones, and thus protect them from neglect by later generations because of their spurious claims to originality.

1

The Person and Society

*Happiness**

It is quite remarkable that utilitarianism should have been most strongly defended by English-speaking writers, whose language is notably deficient in terms by which to convey the delicate shades of meaning required for its adequate elucidation. The need of a milder substitute for *happiness* has been seriously felt, and no doubt serves to obstruct the progress of rational views on this subject. That the defect is in the language and not in the conceptions is evident from the fact that most other languages possess better words. The French *"bonheur"* or the German *"Gluckseligkeit,"* had they their counterpart in English, would afford a delightful relief. [*Dynamic Sociology*]

The idea that happiness is something different from pleasure probably requires no serious refutation. It prevailed formerly because there was supposed to be something essentially bad about pleasure, while happiness was regarded as morally permissible. Now that we know that pleasure is the original good of the sentient world and the essential condition to vital existence, there is no room for anything bad in it, considered in and of itself.

But some will maintain that the idea of pleasure is associated more especially with the sensual feelings, while that of happiness connects itself with the higher emotional ones, and therefore requires special explanation. This is to some extent true, but it is perhaps more correct to define happiness as a condition of continuous or constantly recurring pleasures of whatever class, predominating largely over

* *Dynamic Sociology*, II, p. 147; *Psychic Factors*, Chap. XII, pp. 70–74. See the Preface for full titles and publication data of Ward's writings.

6

pains. It has various degrees from mere contentment to intense enjoyment. Giving the subject an analytical glance, happiness may be seen to require several conditions. The first of these is health. Unless the functions of the body are in harmonious operation nothing worthy of the name happiness can exist. And yet there is an immense difference in the power of different parts of the system to diminish happiness by their derangement. Consumptives are often happy, even buoyant, to the last moment of their lives, while dyspeptics are proverbially wretched, even when their ailment is so slight as to carry no serious menace of death. . . .

. . . . .

The second condition to happiness to be noted is freedom, more or less complete, from pain. To some extent this condition coincides with that of health. For even if we refer to ill-health the accidental external pains due to injury or local diseases, there still remains the most important class of emotional pains—grief, disappointment, worriment, fear, regret, remorse, anxiety, etc., etc. In fact, this list of woes lies only just outside the boundaries of that vast ocean of prurient pains [given] . . . the general name of desires. If any of these remain permanently unsatisfied, happiness is well nigh impossible.

This forms the natural transition to the third and last condition to happiness that need be specially insisted upon, viz., the means of satisfying desire. This is by far the most important of all conditions, because health and freedom from pain are the normal states and their opposites belong to pathology. Their occurrence to a greater or less extent is unavoidable, and we have only nature to blame. This third condition, on the contrary, is, in any state that man has yet attained, comparatively rare, whereas inability to satisfy desire is the almost universal estate of man, and moreover, it is only to a limited extent the fault of nature, and is in the main the fault of social surroundings.

But this needs many qualifications. If only the desires to eat, drink and reproduce were considered, it would indeed be untrue that the means to them were generally wanting. From vast numbers even these are more or less withheld, but such must perish, therefore those that live must possess these primary means of satisfying want. But such satisfactions constitute the lowest grade of happiness, and if the term were not here used in a broad generic sense they would be excluded entirely. Happiness in the popular restricted sense is the experiencing

of the higher emotional pleasures afforded by the gratification of social, esthetic, moral, and intellectual tastes. It is the means of doing
this that render a person, a community, or a nation happy. And these
are constantly arising. New wants of the spiritual nature come thick
and fast upon one another as soon as the coarser necessities of existence are fully supplied. It is really true, as the pessimists claim, that
there is no possibility of satisfying all desires, for if they could all be
once conceived to be satisfied new ones would immediately arise de-
manding satisfaction. Yet the degree of happiness depends upon the
relative proportion of them that can be silenced, and upon the nature
and refinement of the tastes that can be gratified. Therefore, provided
the means of supplying wants can be secured, the greater the number
and the higher the rank of such wants, the higher the state of happiness attainable. The problem of social science is to point out in what
way the most complete and universal satisfaction of human desires
can be attained, and this is one with the problem of greatest happiness. [*Psychic Factors*]

Feeling, Function, and Action*

The two *functions* absolutely essential to life are nutrition and reproduction. To these correspond in all sentient beings two classes
of desires. These may be denominated the *gustatory* and the *sexual*
appetites. By the former, the sustenance necessary for replenishing
the tissues is attracted to its proper place in the system; by the latter,
the reproductive is rendered agreeable, without which it would not
be performed.

Against these objects of nature may be set the corresponding objects of the organism, or, confining ourselves to the human race,
they may be called the objects of man. The end of nature is the
preservation and perpetuation of life; that of man is the satisfaction
of desire. [*Dynamic Sociology*]

. . . Too great stress cannot be laid on the fact that *function is
the object of nature*, in order to bring it into sharp contrast with an-

* *Dynamic Sociology*, I, pp. 468–469; *Psychic Factors*, Chap. XIII, pp. 75–80.

other somewhat new and startling fact, that *feeling is the object of the sentient being.* . . . using the language of evolutionary teleology,* it may be truly said that Nature never intended this to be so. Nature looks upon feeling simply as a means to function. She is utterly indifferent to both pleasure and pain. This is seen in the animal world where one half devour the other half and cruelty and torture are heartlessly practised. It is seen in the human race, half of which is so sunk in hopeless misery that they ceaselessly pray for utter annihilation, and even in the other half there flourishes a philosophy which teaches that to live is to suffer (*leben ist leiden*) and finds no loftier theme than the misery of existence (*Elend des Daseins*).

But in creating pleasure by which to compass her ends Nature, as it were, o'erreached herself. By this act there was brought forth at once the despair and the hope of the world. Designed as a means it at length became an end, and during the last half of the earth's history there has gone on a struggle between Nature and Life for the attainment of their respective ends. Wherever these proved incompatible the end of Life must fail or Life must cease, but in a great number and variety of cases compromise was possible, and the most remarkable consequences ensued. Passing over for the present the subhuman phases of the subject which can be better treated a little later, we come to the human state, and here we find much more clearly defined than ever before this great antithesis between the object of Nature and the object of man. The careful student of man and and of human history easily reaches the generalization that the great drama of human life, like the little drama of each individual life, has for its sole theme the satisfaction of desire. The *dramatis personae* are all seeking to attain some end, to carry some point, to further some scheme, to accomplish some purpose, to gratify some ambition, to realize some aspiration. Or else they are seeking to escape some impending evil, to thwart some vile plot, to defeat some nefarious scheme. There is no end of purposes, some good, some bad, some high, some low, but there is always a purpose. And from the narrow standpoint of self these purposes are all good; that is, they are good for the agent, or, at least, are believed to be so. But this is nothing more than to say that in accomplishing them the agent expects to secure some benefit or escape some injury, i.e., to attain pleasure or avoid pain, or at least, in the ultimate analysis, to realize a balance of

---

* [Evolutionary teleology: literally, gradual goal seeking, or what the Darwinians conceived of as the ultimate end of organic life.]

pleasure or happiness over pain or misery. For the sake of brevity, then, this one universal end of human action and sole object of man may be said to be happiness. The conclusion is thus finally reached that *the object of Nature is function while the object of man is happiness.*

The above will serve as a preparation for considering the third something involved in the satisfaction of desire, which for want of a better term, has been called *action.* Totally distinct in its nature from both feeling and function, it nevertheless invariably accompanies these and mediates between them as the direct consequence of the former, and the necessary condition to the latter. In itself, and except as such consequence and condition, it is utterly useless both to Nature and to the organism. To the former it is simply a mechanical means, to the latter it is a costly burden. Of what use then is it? What intrinsic value has it? To what is it in and for itself an end?

To the answer to these important questions a separate chapter must be devoted, but their full consideration may be anticipated in so far as to premise that for the subhuman world of life, if utility can be predicated of this soulless activity at all, the only beneficiary that can be conceived of is organic progress or evolution. In the human stage, however, this beneficiary assumes a more concrete form and may, without any forced interpretation and in a true and literal sense, be called *Society.*

The threefold truth therefore to which the foregoing considerations growing out of subjective psychology in general and the philosophy of desire in particular have led, is, if we do not descend to the subhuman stage of existence, that:

1. The object of Nature is Function.
2. The object of Man is Happiness.
3. The object of Society is Action. [*Psychic Factors*]

Social Action*

It is the essence of the doctrine of individualism that what is good for the individual must be good for society. This is based on the ad-

* *Psychic Factors*, Chap. XVI, pp. 99–101.

mitted fact that society exists only for the individual. Society is only an idea—a Platonic idea, like species, genus, order, etc., in natural history. The only real thing is the individual. And it is argued: Why strive to benefit that which has no feeling and therefore is incapable of being benefited? The argument is plausible. Only it proceeds from a misconception of what social reformers really mean when they talk of improving society. There are none so simple as literally to personify society and conceive it endowed with wants and passions. By the improvement of society they only mean such modifications in its constitution and structure as will in their opinion result in ameliorating the condition of the individual members. Therefore there is nothing illogical in their claim, and to answer them it must be shown in each case that the particular supposed reform that they are advocating will not as a matter of fact result in the alleged amelioration of the individual members of society. Arguments of this class are legitimate.

It would also be legitimate to argue that no possible alteration in the existing status of society can produce beneficial effects as thus defined, but I am not aware that anyone has ever taken that position. It is too obvious on the most superficial view that the evils that individuals suffer are often due to the constitution of society which entails them. This results from the constant changes that are going on in every direction through the activities of individuals seeking their ends, and from time to time causing the needs of the mass to outgrow the restrictions which society under very different previous circumstances was obliged to impose. So that if a state of perfect adaptation of the individual society could be at any given moment conceived to exist it would not remain so very long, and new internal transformations would soon again throw the individual units out of harmony with the social aggregate. It is this inertia of society and its inability to keep pace with the growth of the living mass within it that gives rise to social reformers who are legitimate and necessary, nay, natural products of every country and age, and the ignoring of this fact by conservative writers who lay so great stress on the word *natural*, is one of the amusing absurdities of the present period.[1]

[1] "*Laissez faire* is 'translated' into 'blunt English' as meaning 'mind your own business,' and this injunction he [Sumner] drives home to almost every one who has ever done anything except to write about 'what social classes owe to each other'; the salutary reservation of Sir Joseph Porter, 'except me,' seeming to be constantly kept in mind. . . .

"Again in his severe condemnation of the 'friends of humanity,' as he sneer-

So long, therefore, as society remains the unconscious product of the individual demands of each age, so long will the organized social state continue to be found out of accord with and lagging behind the real spirit of the age, often so intolerably so as to require more or less violent convulsions and social revolutions. But if ever an ideal social organization shall come to be a clearly defined conscious individual want, it will be possible to establish one that will have elements of flexibility sufficient to render it more or less permanent. But here, as everywhere else under the dominion of the psychic forces, the end of the individual or object of man, happiness, or some improvement in his personal condition, must be put vividly before him as the loadstone of desire and motive to action.

Social Friction[*]

Ethical principles are a growth of the social system. The members of society are literally bound by them, not by an ideal bond, but by positive constraint. The prevailing idea is, that anyone might conduct himself immorally if he preferred, and that pure *principle* is all that prevents the majority of mankind from doing so. Such ideas legitimately follow from the free-will doctrine and other kindred errors that pervade the moral teaching which we all receive. The truth is, that men are compelled to conduct themselves according to the established standards of propriety. This is the condition upon which so-

---

ingly calls all who believe in the attainment through human effort of a higher social state, he seems to forget that these very troublesome persons are merely products of society and *natural*. To hear him, remembering his premises, one would suppose that these men either had invaded the world from some outer planet or had artificially created themselves. But they belong to society as much as the hated paupers and worthless invalids whom he would turn over to nature. Why then not let them alone? Why meddle with the natural course of things? In fact what is the *raison d'être* of this earnest book that wants to have so much done? On his own theory, the author should let his deluded victims alone, should *laissez faire*—we omit the 'translation.' "—Review of Prof. W. G. Sumner's book, entitled: What Social Classes Owe to Each Other. *Man*, Vol. IV; New York, March 1, 1884.

[*] *Dynamic Sociology*, II, pp. 372–373, 376–377, 377–378; *Psychic Factors*, Chap. XVII, pp. 103–115.

ciety has been enabled to develop. The few who attempt to break over these restrictions quickly come to grief. They drop into the criminal classes, and find their way into the penitentiaries; or they are stamped as monomaniacs, fanatics, "cranks," and rigidly guarded. They are driven from the centers of culture, and find for brief periods the means of continuing their licentious course on the expanding borders of civilization. Here they are known as "roughs" and "desperadoes," and flourish until compelled to succumb to the summary justice of "vigilance committees," which are merely the rude guardians of moral law in such communities. For there is really no hard-and-fast line which can be drawn between criminality and the less heinous forms of immorality. But even the least deviation from the path of rectitude is, in developed social centers, a signal for ostracism, the withdrawal of esteem, systematic avoidance, and all the other forms of punishment which render life intolerable, and demonstrate the completely compulsory character of the ethical code. It is a code which enforces itself, and therefore requires no priesthood and no manual. And strangely enough, here, where alone *laissez faire* is sound doctrine, we find the *laissez faire* school calling loudly for "regulation."

. . . . .

The great object of action is to *do* something. Conduct only aims to *avoid doing*—either to avoid interfering with the "pursuits of ends" by others, or to prevent others from pursuing such ends, or to do some benefit for another, whereby he is prevented from doing the necessary acts for rendering an equivalent, or to do him an injury whereby he is prevented, to that extent, from pursuing his natural ends. It is all through a negative proceeding, interfering at every point with the normal course of action. Conduct is a *guidance* of acts so as to prevent or to occasion conflicts in normal actions.

. . . . .

Moral conduct, instead of being, as usually represented, conduct in a right line, is in reality conduct in a very irregular line. The path of *rectitude* is a crooked path, and the distance lost in following it counts heavily against the progress of the world, yet less heavily than would the jars and collisions which a failure to follow it would inevitably produce.

The remarkable fact to be noted is, that it is this class of human action, aiming simply to avoid such conflicts of interest, insignificant as it is in comparison with the main current of human action, that has been the subject of all the ethical teaching and ethical writing which have flooded the world from the earliest historic periods. [*Dy-namic Sociology*]

If any one were to write a book professing its title to set forth the value of machinery and its usefulness to civilization, and were to confine himself exclusively to the subject of friction, pointing out in great detail the importance of reducing it to the minimum, describing the most effective kinds of journals, gudgeons, and bearings for this purpose, and treating exhaustively the subject of lubricating oils, the case would be closely analogous to that which exists with respect to the treatment by all writers of human or social action. Unquestionably the most important subject that can engage the attention of the human mind, its laws, principles and methods, as well as its substantial results have been ignored and volumes by thousands have been written on the mere friction which it engenders, its interferences and conflicts and how they may be lessened. This insignificant field of investigation has been dignified by the high-sounding name of ethics, or sometimes even by the more grandiloquent one of "moral science." These voluminous reports of the Circumlocution Office upon "the art of perceiving how not to do it" are a piece with the traditional schoolboy's composition on pins setting forth their usefulness in saving men's lives by their not swallowing them.

That unthinking persons, theological writers, and authors of sentimental homilies should extol morals and regard it as the chief end of life is not perhaps to be wondered at; but that philosophers of breadth and penetration should have so uniformly failed to assign it its proper and natural place in their systems, will always remain one of the curiosities of the human mind. It would at least be supposed that where one of these latter was also a professed teacher of social science, and as such to have been forced to make the most careful study and analysis of all the different kinds of social action, he could not help seeing the subordinate rank and incidental character of those negative phenomena which alone belong to ethics. It is all the more surprising, therefore to find Mr. Herbert Spencer making this subject to form the cap-sheaf and crown of this great system of synthetic philosophy, and speaking of that part of his system as the one to which he regards "all the preceding parts as subsidiary."

While sociology deals with all human actions and, therefore, includes ethics, the latter deals only with the limited class of actions which are properly included under the word *conduct*, and which, as said above, constitute the conflicts that occur in normal action. They are not only unimportant from their limited scope, but from their essentially negative character. Their tendency, as in mechanical friction, is to impede, and to their full extent, to prevent the regular operations of society. They are therefore wholly non-progressive. Any one who from moral considerations acts in any respect differently from what the psychic forces within him normally impel him to act, to that extent lessens the effect of his action. Of course this is far from saying that it is not very frequently necessary and in all respects best to do this, it is merely to insist that there is nothing so wonderful and exalted about moral acts as is commonly supposed, when viewed from the broadest philosophical standpoint. If one sees the question only from the standpoint of social progress, which consists in producing the maximum permanent improvements in man's material surroundings, all hindrances to this consummation are bad, and those acts which are morally good are in most instances socially bad.

It may be admitted that the subject of interferences among human actions and of their avoidance is a complex and difficult one, nevertheless it has been so long and exhaustively studied that it seems impossible to add anything of value. All the great moral precepts are as old as human records. The "golden rule" of Christ was laid down independently by Hillel and Confucius and never practiced by any one. Among the best maxims are those of the Brahmins, while Antoninus and the Stoics have furnished as pure and lofty conceptions of duty as any modern moral science writer could wish. Mr. Spencer laid claim to finding a "scientific basis" for ethics. One volume of his Principles of Ethics is now out and I am unable to see that he has sustained that claim if by "scientific basis" he means anything else than the old basis. What he says that is new is not part of ethics. The doctrine that pleasure is the good and pain the bad, and that happiness is the end of action, while "scientific" is not ethical. It is a corollary dimly seen by Spinoza and others, growing out of the principle set forth in Chap. VII, which is a principle of psychology, or, one may say, of biology. And as to his "Justice" the subject does not belong to ethics, but to jurisprudence. As treated by him it is a partisan defence of extreme individualism, amounting to practical anarchism.

However important moral conduct may be in itself, and there is no difference of opinion on this point, there are many reasons, in its overdone condition already referred to, why it should not be made to absorb so large a share of the attention of thinking persons. The moral precepts observed at any time and in any country are the effect and not the cause of the moral condition of those who observe them. If there is any mutual interaction between ethical teaching and moral conduct by which each influences the other and tends to cause the advance of both it is very slight. Certain it is that the former can be and frequently is pushed so far the moral sense is more or less blunted and deadened by the iteration of moral injunctions. It would probably be better for personal morality if ethics were only taught historically and philosophically.

Another serious evil results from the erroneous belief that moral character can be improved by ethical teaching. Many persons, and especially teachers, habitually labor under such a load of responsibility for the moral character of those who come within the circle of their influence that they become paralyzed for usefulness in life. No one dares to say what he thinks. All originality is screened out of whatever is produced. Teaching, that noblest of all vocations, degenerates into pedantry. This has now reached such a stage that the utterances of professors in colleges have assumed a stereotyped form and the sagacious student knows in advance what is going to be said. Or, if any one of these should chance to say anything original, he feels obliged immediately to recant it, or to add a saving clause to the effect that he meant something else. And it is getting to be the practice in set papers, orations, and scholastic addresses in which the mind has been allowed some freedom to expand, to close with a "protest," as the Catholic writers call it, namely a disclaimer of everything that could be construed to be injurious to morals. Frequently, after stating an important scientific truth, it is deemed necessary to explain to the readers, as the judge does to the jury, how much of it it will do to believe and what conclusions it will not do to draw from it. University lectures become infected with this true moral cowardice, until the lecture-room style can be recognized and readily distinguished from the independent exposition of the original investigator. The same difference is seen in the books produced by the two classes, in the cringing fear that animates the one, contrasted with the manly courage characterizing the other.

Along with the dwarfing effect of this state of things, there goes the further demoralizing influence of egotism and conceit. For the idea of continually guarding the character of others begets an inordinate

conception of personal importance, and this is always seen gro-
tesquely mixing itself with pretended humility. A form of this sometimes takes possession even of truly great minds, and unless checked
by wholesome influences from without they are apt to merge into a
state in which they vastly overestimate the effect their labors are to
produce. It was so with Auguste Comte, after long practising his
"hygiene cerebrale" of reading nothing and conversing with no one,
but evolving his system out of his inner consciousness, until he fan-
cied himself the high priest of a new dispensation and even fixed the
time for its universal acceptance. And do we not see some trace of
this enlarged personality in Mr. Herbert Spencer when, in the preface
to his Data of Ethics, he explains his haste to lay before the world
his ethical system before any serious evils should result from its delay?
For it is in this connection that he says: "Few things can happen
more disastrous than the decay and death of a regulative system no
longer fit, before another and fitter regulative system has grown up
to replace it." Under such a weight of responsibility he ought at least
to be consoled by the view expressed in this chapter and to congratu-
late himself that the morals of the world may still be safe even if he
should not live to complete his Principles of Ethics.

To all this may now be added the further law that the moral state
is a product of social evolution and a condition to the existence of
society. The moral code only differs from the legal code in taking
cognizance of cases that society will adjudicate without the aid of the
courts. Society will not tolerate an incorrigibly immoral member. To
be in society at all and out of jail he must practice the moral virtues
of his age and country. Great latitude there no doubt is in these
matters, but his treatment by his fellow men will depend upon the
degree to which he conforms to popular conceptions of right, and
though he may keep within legal rules, if he persists in violating moral
rules he will be ostracized and deprived of the means of gaining a
livelihood, and ultimately made to perish and make room for those
who will conform. Therefore there is no need to preach morality. It
is self-regulating. Society literally compels its members to observe its
moral laws.

To the statement that ethics merely represents the social friction
it may be objected that this is to take too narrow a view of the subject,
that there are departments of ethics that are not covered by this
definition. I have tried to discover such and thus far failed, although
there are some cases in which this is apparently true. It may be said

that ethics need not necessarily relate to others, but may relate wholly to self. One may do an immoral act to himself wholly irrespective of any other individual. For example he may be intemperate and thus abuse his own nature. To this it may be replied that if he were alone in some vast wilderness and his act were unknown to any other human being this would be a case in point. But it is merely a hypothetical case which could practically never occur, and if it should occur it would have no importance, because such a life would be socially useless. But the moment he is brought into society his immoral practices begin to react on others and in various ways to increase the friction of the social machinery.

It is also true that this view relates primarily to normal or egoistic conduct and only secondarily to supranormal or altruistic, better named *supererogatory* conduct. At least beneficence, benevolence, philanthropy, charity, etc., do not directly result from conflicts in normal action. But we have only to analyze the motives to these to perceive that they are at least the indirect consequences of such conflicts. Taking charitable acts as the generic type of the whole supererogatory class, it is obvious that they presuppose the prior existence in society of serious obstructions to the normal course of action. They exist only because there is a class in society who are in some way more or less deprived of the means of subsistence. How came such a class to exist? Clearly through some form of interference with their normal actions. There is an abundance of food. The benevolent class possess a large enough surplus. Those who have nothing, were they free to act, would proceed to supply themselves with the surplus. Something prevents them from doing so. It is not to the purpose to inquire here what the nature of these barriers is, it is only necessary to point out that they exist. But this is only to say that action has been interfered with, arrested, clogged, choked, and hence objects of charity exist in society. An act of charity is, therefore, from our present standpoint, simply a mode, usually only a temporary one, of relieving pressure upon this class, of clearing away the obstructions to life, in a word, of overcoming the social friction.

The above is independent of the ethical nature of this kind of social friction and also of that of charitable action in general. It is fashionable now-a-days to animadvert upon all charitable work from the supposed fundamental and scientific standpoint that it interferes with the law of the survival of the fittest in society. The argument proceeds from a superficial analogy between animal life and human life, and is neither scientific nor sound. But this much is true and is the basis of the popular error, namely that under the law of parsimony, i.e., that an individual will always seek the greatest gain for the least effort, it is easy to create a pauper class by injudicious charity. This class then becomes in society the strict homologue of the degenerate parasite so well known in almost every department of biology.

There is, however, a really fundamental and scientific objection to charity, but this I have never seen stated. It is that charity is really the giving by the benevolent class, not to the indigent class, but to the non-benevolent class. To illustrate this let us take the case of waiters' "tips" and porters' fees. All who have ever given the subject a moment's thought know that to tip a waiter or fee a porter is simply to give so much money to a hotel keeper or a railroad company. Its effect is to encourage these to continue to keep down the wages of these employes to the point of dependence upon the public, and the more generous the public the lower will be the wages. If all would resolve to cease tipping and feeing altogether, these employes would be paid regular wages like other employes. Charity and almsgiving do not differ in principle from this giving of tips and fees. It is true that in the latter case it is definitely known from whom the money should be taken as an act of justice, while in the former case the ones who should pay it are a large ill-defined class. But there is no doubt that the ones who have the wealth of the world have included in it the share of those who have none. The only escape from this conclusion is to say, as many are ready to do, that those who have nothing have no right to exist in society. If the indigent class were coextensive and identical with the criminal class there would be some ground for this position. But those who assume it generally argue that the poor are more moral than the rich, and it is probably true that the percentage of criminals from the wealthy classes is greater than that from the indigent classes. The only argument remaining is that poverty is due to idleness and profligacy. Yet if the percentage of idle and profligate rich could be compared with that of the idle and profligate poor, it would make a far worse showing for the former than that of the comparative criminality of these two classes. The conclusion therefore remains unassailable that the means of subsistence is justly due to the indigent class from the opulent class, and no amount of patchwork on the part of a few benevolent persons can ever balance this great account with society. Its effect is to increase the surplus of the non-benevolent in the sums contributed by the benevolent.

The several considerations above brought forward are merely samples of the short-sighted and superficial character of nearly everything that is said or done with relation to ethics. This is because in the nature of things there cannot be any logical and fundamental treatment of that subject. The moment logic and scientific principles are applied the problem ceases to be an ethical one and becomes a sociological one. The ethical and sociological standpoints are the opposites of each other. The former looks to the curbing, the latter to the freeing of social energy. Any philosophy that has for its object the hemming and cribbing of a great natural force can have no permanence. As well try to dam the waters of a river and hope for final success.

This thought introduces the fundamental truth with which this treatment of social friction must conclude. It is that the whole subject of ethics is essentially provisional and the stage to which it belongs is a merely transitional stage. There are those who by devoting their whole lives to doing good conceive of the life of future blessedness as one in which there shall be no other occupation but that of doing good. They forget that they have been taught that in that life there will be no one to need their ministrations. Could they realize such a state it would appear a wretched one. The only thing they enjoy they would be deprived of. I have known saintly beings of this class who seemed so to long for an opportunity to do good, that they could not conceal a secret joy at the occurrence of an unfortunate accident which promised to furnish such an opportunity. Were all suffering abolished the occupation of such persons would be gone. And yet Mr. Spencer and other ethical writers do but reflect a widespread popular sentiment in regarding ethical conduct as the climax of human achievement and ethics as the goal of philosophy.

The idea that there must always be a field for ethical action is only a part of the more general idea that all things must always be what they now are. And both of these ideas prevail in the face of the fact that the most radical changes have actually many times taken place within the narrow limits of human history. "The poor always ye have with you" is supposed to express a necessary social truth. It is doubtless as true now as it was two thousand years ago, but that is far from giving warrant for saying that it will continue to be true two thousand years hence. There are many who think that it will have ceased to be true two hundred years hence. But if it shall thus cease it will not be ethical teaching but improved social organization that will have produced the change. And so one might take up one by one all the

social facts that make ethical conduct possible, and theoretically conceive of their elimination. It will, of course, be said that such an idea
is visionary and utopian. Grant this and it still remains true that if
any of the existing evils can be removed the domain of ethics is to
that extent circumscribed. Deny that this is possible and the utility
of all ethical work is given over. Admit that it is possible and there
is no place to stop short of a reclamation of the whole field.

But is this claim wholly utopian? Has there been no moral progress?
If not why continue to inculcate moral principles? As a matter of fact
there has been great moral progress. Let any one read the history of
England, even the meager account of its kings and their exploits
which is called history, and compare the acts of the men of the 12th
to the 16th centuries with those of the men occupying relatively the
same national and social positions today, and see whether there has
been any moral progress. Not even in Russia which we call despotic
is there anything to compare with the immorality that openly stalked
abroad three hundred years ago over all Europe. The subject need
not be enlarged upon. The other point to be noted is that none of
this real moral progress has been due to the enforcement and inculca-
tion of moral precepts. It has been wholly due to the march of events,
such as the growth of scientific ideas, the spread of letters, the influence of commerce, the establishment of universities, the invention
of printing, and the introduction of machinery and manufactures; in
general to the progress of intelligence, laying bare the enormity of the
abuses formerly practised and creating a new code of morals which
society literally enforces. Men could not be as cruel and immoral as
they once were if they would. The power of public sentiment crushes
every display of it. In other words as already stated, the modern improved morality is a condition to the modern improved state of civilization and the latter is the cause of the former, not the reverse as
ethical expounders teach.

The effect of social friction is always painful, therefore moral progress, which consists in reducing this friction, is restricted in its popular acceptation to the lessening of pain, i.e., to the mitigation of suffering, the decrease of misery, and the removal of unhappiness in general. In short it is negative in its character, and such it really is in the
main. But there may be a positive moral progress consisting in the
increase of pleasure, the heightening of enjoyment, and the broaden-
ing and deepening of human happiness. Just as social friction is painful so social action is pleasurable. All desire is for the exercise of some

function, and the objects of desire are such only by virtue of making such exercise possible. Happiness therefore can only be increased by increasing either the number or the intensity of satisfiable desires. It has in fact been greatly increased in both these ways. Without elaborating this principle I will simply point to the very modern date of two of the highest sources of man's present enjoyment in civilized countries, the enjoyment of music and the enjoyment of what may be called beauty in the amorphous—in the landscape, the clouds, the sea, the rocks, and the mountains. No faculty for appreciating either of these sources of delight seemed to exist in what we call ancient times, and it is practically wanting in all but modern civilized races. At least it cannot be sufficiently developed elsewhere to make up any considerable part of their enjoyment of life, which is the present point of view. Yet its germs doubtless exist in all races and have existed at all times, capable of development through civilization.

The highest ideal of happiness, therefore, is the freest exercise of the greatest number and most energetic faculties. This must also be the highest ethical ideal. But it is clear that its realization would abolish moral conduct altogether and remove the very field of ethics from a scheme of philosophy. To remove the obstacles to free social activity is to abolish the so-called science of ethics. The avowed purpose of ethics is to abolish itself. The highest ethics is no ethics. Ideally moral conduct is wholly unmoral conduct. Or more correctly stated, the highest ideal of a moral state is one in which there will exist nothing that can be called moral.

Whether we look at the subject from the standpoint of social progress or from that of individual welfare the liberation of social energy is the desideratum. The sociologist demands it because it increases the progressive power of society. The moralist should demand it because it increases happiness. For activity means both, and therefore the more activity the better. True morality not less than true progress consists in the emancipation of social energy and the free exercise of power. Evil is merely the friction which is to be overcome or at least minimized. This cannot be done by exhortation. It must be done by perfecting the social mechanism. The tendencies that produce evil are not in themselves evil. There is no absolute evil. None of the propensities which now cause evil are essentially bad. They are all in themselves good, must necessarily be so, since they have been developed for the sole purpose of enabling man to exist, survive, and progress. All evil is relative. Any power may do harm.

The forces of nature are good or bad according to where they are permitted to expend themselves. The wind is evil when it dashes the vessel on the rocks; it is good when it fills the sail and speeds it on its way. Fire is evil when it rages through a great city and destroys life and property; it is good when it warms human dwellings or creates the wondrous power of steam. Electricity is evil when in the thunderbolt it descends from the cloud and scatters death and destruction; it is good when it transmits messages of love to distant friends. And so it is with the passions of men as they surge through society. Left to themselves like the physical elements they find vent in all manner of ways and constantly dash against the interests of those who chance to be in their way. But like the elements they readily yield to the touch of true science, which directs them into harmless, nay, useful channels, and makes them instruments for good. In fact human desires . . . seeking their satisfaction through appropriate activity, constitute the only good from the standpoint of sociology. They are the *Social Forces.* [*Psychic Factors*]

Economy of Nature and Mind*

. . . Increasing density of population, as all know, by the friction it produces of mind with mind, tends of itself to sharpen the wits and increase that practical form of intelligence which counts in the struggle for existence. But along with this there has gone an immense increase in the educational facilities offered in cities. Not to mention the improved public school system and lengthened terms of general study with the high schools added on, some of which fit their pupils for entering college, there are the multiplied business and commercial colleges specially adapted to teach young people how to transact business, conduct enterprises, and in general to "make money."

Notwithstanding all the hollow cant about the "dignity of labor," to work with one's hands in any productive occupation is looked upon by all as degrading, and those who do so are denied all social position. To avoid this worst of all conditions and live by his wits or

* *Psychic Factors*, Chap. XXXIII, pp. 272–273, 275–276, 278–279.

by some of the more genteel and less debasing occupations is the supreme effort of every "intelligent" person. The effect is to throng the
"learned professions" with aspirants to this honor; multiply the town
lawyers, attorneys, constables, notaries, justices, and "officers"; breed
swarms of real estate agents, insurance agents, bankers, brokers and
shavers; overdo all newspaper and literary enterprises; develop a vast
army of reporters, stenographers, typewriters, and copyists; and make
everyone fit himself to be at least a clerk, or something besides a
mere laborer, mechanic, or artisan. Immensely overdone as all these
departments are, they still manage to exist and flourish, and they do
this by increasing the cost of the products to the maximum limit at
which the public will use them. How competition of this class can
be kept up under such influences is well shown by the number of
"first class restaurants" in all large cities, feeding only a few accidental
stragglers or wealthy persons, and where one seems to be paying almost exclusively for the costly silverware and mostly idle retinue of
attendants.

. . . . .

While competition is not to be looked upon as a social desideratum,
even in its pure animal form, much less in its aggressive human form,
free individual activity under the full play of all natural motives is
of the utmost importance. Among these motives those of friendly
rivalry and honest emulation are legitimate, harmless, and powerful.
These competition suppresses; it tends to choke individual freedom
and clog the wheels of social progress. How can this true individualism be secured and complete freedom of individual action be vouch-
safed? Herein lies a social paradox. It is clear from what has been said
that this will never bring itself about. The tendencies are strongly in
the opposite direction. Competition is growing more and more aggressive, heated, and ephemeral. Combination is growing more and
more universal, powerful and permanent. This is the result of the
most complete *laissez faire* policy. The paradox therefore is that *individual freedom can only come through social regulation.* The coopera-
tive effects of the rule of mind which annihilate competition can only
be overcome by that still higher form of cooperation which shall stay
the lower form and set free the normal faculties of man. Free competition that shall be both innocent and beneficial may be secured to
a limited extent in this way and in another way.

As a single illustration of this, let us suppose a railroad to be constructed alongside of an existing canal. Negotiations will be at once

set on foot on the part of the railroad company to purchase the canal, not because it is wanted, but merely to remove it from competition. Such negotiations would be sure to succeed and leave the railroad master of the field. Competition would be removed, rates of transportation increased, and a valuable water way would be abandoned. But suppose society in its collective capacity, however constituted, seeing the situation and the danger, were to step in and itself purchase the canal, and to continue in spite of the railroad to conduct it in the interest of traffic; here would be a case in which the law of mind would be directed to maintaining instead of destroying competition.

A new and revised political economy will doubtless be largely devoted to showing, not so much the glories of competition, which society does not enjoy, as how society may conduct itself in order to secure whatever benefits competition can offer, and also how the competition that cannot be prevented can be shorn of its wasteful and aggressive features. Neither should the higher attributes of reason and intelligence be discouraged. They represent the true elements of civilization and progress. But these, too, should be deprived of their fangs. The way to counteract the evil effects of mind operating in the individual is to infuse a larger share of the same mind element into the controlling power of society. Such a powerful weapon as reason is unsafe in the hands of one individual when wielded against another. It is still more dangerous in the hands of corporations, which proverbially have no souls. It is most baneful of all in the hands of compound corporations which seek to control the wealth of the world. It is only safe when employed by the social ego, emanating from the collective brain of society, and directed toward securing the common interests of the social organism.

. . . . .

Economic Paradoxes:

1. Subsistence increases instead of diminishing with population (reversal of the Malthusian dictum).

2. The interest of the individual is rarely the same as that of society.

3. Owing to ignorance of the remote effects of actions men do not always do what is for their own interests.

4. Cheapness is a stronger inducement than quality, and the consumer cannot be depended upon to encourage the better producer.

5. Competition raises prices and rates.

6. Combination often lowers prices and rates.

7. Free competition is only possible under social regulation.

8. Private monopoly can only be prevented by public monopoly.

9. The hope of gain is not always the best motive to industry.

10. Public service will secure better talent than private enterprise for the same outlay.

11. Market values and social values are not identical.

12. The prosperity of a community depends as much upon the mode of consumption as upon the quantity produced.

13. Private enterprise taxes the people more heavily than government.

14. The social effects of taxation are more important than its fiscal effects.

15. The producer cannot always shift the burden of taxation upon the consumer, e.g., under monopoly and aggressive competition.

16. Protection may reduce the price of the commodity protected, not only in the protecting but even in the importing country.

17. Capital, as embodied in machinery, contributes more than labor to the production of wealth.

18. Wages are drawn from products and not from capital, and the "wage-fund" is a myth.

19. Increase of wages is attended with increase of profits.

20. Prices fall as wages rise.

21. Diminished hours of labor bring increased production.

22. Reduction of the time worked enhances the wages received.

23. A man working alone earns the same as when his wife and children also work.

24. Lowering the rate of interest may lead to increased savings.

The Social Intellect*

But should . . . all the practical knowledge of the world be given to every member of society for his guidance, there would still remain, especially during the transition period before such a measure could bear its full fruit, a wide field for the exercise of the collective inge-

* *Psychic Factors,* Chap. XXXVII, pp. 308–312.

nuity. As happiness is the great object of man, the problem before
the social intellect is nothing less than that of the organization of
happiness. The existing evils of society are so great and so universal
that the first steps would necessarily be taken rather in the direction
of mitigating or removing these than in that of increasing or extend-
ing the positive enjoyment of life. So long as there is pain to be re-
lieved, the attempt to heighten pleasure seems a sacrilege. The social
intellect should, therefore, first and foremost, grapple with the whole
problem of reducing the social friction. Every wheel in the entire
social machinery should be carefully scrutinized with the practiced
eye of the skilled artisan, with a view to discovering the true nature
of the friction and of removing all that is not required by a perfect
system.

With regard to the method by which all this may be made prac-
ticable a final word may be indulged in. Before any such sweeping
social regeneration as that which is here hinted at can be inaugurated
a great change must be wrought in the whole theory of legislation.
It must be recognized that the legislator is essentially an inventor and
a scientific discoverer. His duty is to be thoroughly versed in the whole
theory and practice of social physics. He is called upon to devise
"ways and means" for securing the true interests and improvement
of the people for whom he is to legislate. This obviously cannot be
done by existing methods. A public assembly governed by parliamen-
tary rules is as inadequate a method as could well be conceived of for
anything like scientific legislation. Imagine all the inventors in the
country assembled in a hall acting under the gavel of a presiding
officer to devise the machines of the future and adopt the best by
a majority vote! Or think of trying to advance scientific discovery by
a general convention! Scientific associations there are, usually for the
reading of papers setting forth the discoveries made by the members
in their laboratories, and there would be no objection to this class of
legislative assemblies. But in the latter case as in the former, the real
work, the thought, research, observation, experimentation, and discovery of laws and principles of nature must be done elsewhere, under
appropriate conditions, in the great field or in the private cabinet.

It may at first glance seem absurd to propose that legislation be
done in any such way, but a little reflection will show that it is not
only not absurd, but that there is at this moment a strong tendency
in all enlightened countries toward its adoption. It is a well known
fact that at the present time the greater part of the real legislation is

done by committees. The members of legislative committees are carefully chosen with reference to their known fitness for the different
subjects intrusted to them. These committees really *deliberate*. They
investigate the questions before them, hear testimony and petitions,
and weigh evidence for and against every proposed measure. This is
truly scientific and leads to the discovery of the principles involved.
Unless biased by partisan leanings they are very likely to reach the
truth and report practical and useful measures. The body to which
these committees belong respect their decisions and usually adopt
their recommendations. The other members usually know very little
about the merits of the questions, or at least, not having studied them,
they defer to the superior judgment of those who have. Committee
work is, therefore, the nearest approach we have to the scientific
investigation of social questions. It is on the increase, and is destined
to play an ever increasing role in national legislation.

There is one other important way in which the social intellect is
being applied to human affairs. The theory is that the executive
branch of government merely administers national affairs. This is a
great mistake. A very large part of the real legislation of a country
is done by the executive branch. The various bureaus of government
are in a position to feel the popular pulse more sensitively than the
legislature. The officers charged with their administration become
identified with certain industries and are appealed to by the public
to adopt needed reforms. After stepping to the verge of their legal
authority in response to such demands, whereby much real legislation is done not contemplated by those who framed the laws under
which these bureaus were established, they finish by making recommendations of the rest to the law-making power. This latter usually
recognizes the wisdom of such recommendations and enacts them
into laws, thus ever enlarging the administrative jurisdiction of government. Such legislation is in a true sense scientific. It is based on
a knowledge both of the needs of the public and of the best means
of supplying them. It has been subjected to thoughtful consideration
and mature judgment. It is a method that is being every year more
and more employed, and its results are usually successful and permanent.

History furnishes the statesman an additional basis for legislation.
It is now possible to acquire a knowledge of the industrial history of
nations, not complete, it is true, because so much was lost during the
period when history was supposed to relate exclusively to the opera-

tions of the state and those who stood at its head, but sufficiently full to serve as a valuable guide to the legislator. No man should consider himself qualified to legislate for a people who is not conversant with the history of modern nations at least, with their various systems of finance, revenue, taxation, public works, education, land surveying, patent and copyright law, military and naval equipment, general jurisprudence and constitutional, statute, and unwritten law. It will, of course, be said that very few legislators are thus informed, and this is true, but these few will be the ones who will do most to shape the action of the state and will furnish examples to all who aspire to play a leading part in the political drama.

Again there is the statistical method. No one will deny that this is rapidly becoming a leading factor in legislation. Statistics are simply the facts that underlie the science of government. They are to the legislator what the results of observation and experiment are to the man of science. They are in fact the inductions of political science, and the inductive method in that science is of the same value that it is to science in general, its only true foundation. There is no great state at this day that does not make an effort to collect statistics; in most of the leading nations of the world this is now done on an extensive scale. A census, which a short time ago was merely an enumeration of the population of a state, now means an exhaustive inquiry into its entire vital, industrial, and commercial condition. In this and many other ways governments furnish to their legislators the most important facts required to guide them in the adoption of the measures needful for the prosperity of the people.

There are many other ways in which the tendency toward scientific legislation is steadily growing, and, without indulging in any undue optimism on the subject, the fact may be considered established that no revolution is necessary in the character of society in order to bring about the gradual transformation required to realize all that has been foreshadowed in this chapter. The machinery already exists for the needed reformation and all that is necessary is that it be under the control of the developed social intellect. The quality of statesmanship is increasing. More thought is being devoted to the deeper questions of state and of society than ever before, and the signs of healthy progress are unmistakable. A modern Solon, paraphrasing the oft-quoted saying of the ancient one, has defined a statesman as "a successful politician who is dead." He doubtless intended to rebuke the tendency of every age to vilify public men while they are living and

Social Patterns of Behavior

General Characteristics of
Pure Sociology*

We cannot too strongly emphasize the paradox that pure science really rests on *faith*. "Faith . . . that causation is universal." Faith not only that all effects have causes but also that all causes have effects; faith that whatever is is worthy, and that whatever is worth being is worth knowing; and finally faith, since this cannot be wholly suppressed, that some beneficial result will follow the discovery of truth. But this faith need not go so far as to become anthropocentric and optimistic, so as to divert the investigator from the single pursuit of truth and carry him off in a vain search for the supposed necessary uses of facts or for strained analogies and imaginary harmonies.

Another reef to be shunned is the notion that was formerly quite prevalent and which is still continually coming into view, that science consists in the discovery of facts. There is not a single science of which this is true, and a much more nearly correct definition would be that science consists in reasoning about facts. This is perhaps best illustrated in geology, where the facts—rocks—are infinitely older than human history or the human race, and most of them have stared the world in the face throughout all ages, but were never *known* till men began to reason about them and interpret them. But the truth comes nearer home in the more practical sciences like physics and chemistry. The forces of nature and the properties of substances have always existed, but they were of comparatively little use until the age of experimentation which involves the closest reasoning. The electricity

* *Pure Sociology*, Chap. I, p. 6.

that lights our houses and propels our cars was here all the time, and could just as well have been used two thousand or four thousand years ago as now, if any one had thought out and worked out its true nature, as has so recently been done.

Subject-Matter of Sociology *

If achievement consisted in wealth, the objects of production would have grown more and more durable with the progress of civilization. The fact is precisely the reverse of this. Whatever class of objects we may examine, we find that the farther back we go the more solid and enduring the materials are of which they are constructed. This is perhaps the most strikingly exemplified in architecture. Compare the old with the new part of any city of Europe, or even of America. I once engaged a room in a house on Essex Street, Strand, of which the front door consisted of ponderous planks six inches thick. The enlightened host apologized for it, saying that it was a very old house. Without some such experience, the modern American law student can scarcely understand the phrase he finds in his "Blackstone," that in English law "a man's house is his castle." The clapboarded balloon frames of the Middle West are more like "castles in the air." But any American who has seen Europe, even in the capacity of a tourist, knows that this case was no particular exception. Builders in European cities have unlimited difficulty in trying to introduce into the older buildings such "modern improvements" as water and gas pipes, and electric wires. Such buildings were built to stay, and many of them are still very strong. But to see the perishability of even such structures it is only necessary to visit such castles and chateaus as those of Colchester or Shinon. But there has been a gradual change in the character of architecture, both public and private, in the direction of less and less solidity, durability and costliness, from the pyramids of Egypt to the cottages of modern summer resorts.

Not less clearly is this tendency illustrated by the history of bookmaking since the invention of printing. Any one who has had occasion to handle books published in the sixteenth or seventeenth century,

* *Applied Sociology*, Chap. III, pp. 24–26.

does not need to have this point further enforced. Often printed on parchment, always with strong, almost indestructible binding, firmly and securely hand sewed, not to speak of the elaborate ornamentation of the title page and rubrics at the heads of chapters, these ancient tomes are the embodiments of painstaking workmanship and durability. Contrast them with modern books. Four centuries hence there will scarcely exist a copy of a nineteenth-century book that anybody reads. Many an *edition de luxe* even will go to pieces on the shelves of public libraries.

But to these qualities of durability and expensiveness have succeeded those of ready reproduction and indefinite multiplication. These are the elements of diffusion and popularization. It is an evening up of conditions. For along with the massive structures, chiefly for tombs of dead rulers or temples to the gods, there went great deprivation, even in the means of shelter, for the living men of the time. So, too, in the early history of book-making, only the very few could afford to own a book. Only the cheap can become universal, and it is easier to renew a cheap article than to guard a costly one. The ages of stone and bronze and iron have successively passed, and we are living in an age of paper and caoutchouc.

Achievement does not consist in wealth. Wealth is fleeting and ephemeral. Achievement is permanent and eternal. And now mark the paradox. Wealth, the transient, is material; achievement, the enduring, is immaterial. The products of achievement are not material things at all. As said before, they are not ends but means. They are methods, ways, principles, devices, arts, systems, institutions. In a word, they are *inventions*. Achievement consists in invention in the Tardean sense. It is anything and everything that rises above mere imitation or repetition. Every such increment to civilization is a permanent gain, because it is imitated, repeated, perpetuated, and never lost. It is chiefly mental or psychical, but it may be physical in the sense of skill. The earlier developments of civilizing influences consisted mainly in these, and such accounts as we have consist in descriptions of the physical feats of heroes. But mere muscular strength soon yields to cunning and skill. These do not achieve until they begin to create. Language itself was an achievement of stupendous import, and every one of the steps it has taken—gesture, oral, written, printed forms of language—has marked an epoch in the progress of man. Literature has become one of the great achievements. Art, too, is an achievement upon which we need not dwell. Philosophy and

science must be ranked as achievements, vast and far-reaching in their
consequences. The invention of tools, instruments, utensils, missiles,
traps, snares, and weapons comes under this head, crowned by the
era of machino-facture, artificial locomotion, and electric intercom-
munication.

Methodology *

Not only are the common wants of men the same, but their passions are also the same, and those acts growing out of them which are
regarded as destructive of the social order and condemned by law and
public opinion are committed in the face of these restraining influences with astonishing regularity. This is not seen by the ordinary
observer, and every crime or breach of order is commonly looked
upon as exceptional and arouses great local or general interest according to its nature and the circumstances attending it. But when accu-
rate statistics are brought to bear upon this class of social phenomena
they prove to be quite as uniform, though not quite so frequent, as
the normal operations of life. Even the most extraordinary occur-
rences, such as the killing of an aged parent by a child or the marriage
of brother and sister, actually occur once in about so long, or so as to
form a certain percentage of the homicides or marriages. There is a
law of deviation from a mean, upon which Galton lays great stress,
which explains such cases. . . . Fanatics illustrate an aspect of it.
When any question agitates the public mind there is a great central
mass of men who take an ordinary enlightened interest in it. Below
these there is a body of persons experiencing an interest diminishing
in degree until it practically vanishes. Above the mean there is a
certain number with whom the interest is greater, and this rises with
diminishing numbers until there is reached a point at which a very
few persons are wholly engrossed in the question. There may be one
so completely absorbed as to be capable of committing a terrible
crime, such as assassination. This is probably the true psychological
explanation of all three of the presidential assassinations in the United
States. Such acts might be represented geometrically as forming the

* *Pure Sociology*, Chap. IV, pp. 54–55.

apex of a curve, or the maximum deviation from the mean. Even assassinations are regular social phenomena, as any one may see by casting a glance backward through less than half a century. This does not mean that they cannot and should not be prevented by every power society possesses, nor does it mean that any crime may not be utterly eradicated by appropriate social action. In fact all history proves that the forces underlying crime, as well as many actions that are not criminal, have been gradually drawn off into other channels, or in scientific phrase, commuted, by civilizing agencies.

Biologic Origins of
the Subjective Faculties[*]

We may therefore probably say with some approach toward the truth that the object of nature, as this phrase has been explained, is to convert as large an amount as possible of inorganic into organic and organized matter. This may be a somewhat unpoetical conclusion, and if we could have things as we want them a more delicate and respectable end might be imagined for nature to pursue. But we are only trying to ascertain what the end really is toward which things tend, and this formula comes nearer to expressing it than any other that has been offered. It may be asked why the end is not rather structural perfection. But this, as we have seen, seems to be a means rather than an end. It obviously accomplishes the end, and it seems to be a more pertinent question how it happened to be hit upon as a means. And here we encounter a curious state of things which we shall find to recur at almost every one of the great cosmic steps. Weismann several times refers to certain peculiar phenomena which he meets with in the course of his biological researches, for which there seems to have been no antecedent preparation, and which in the normal course of things would not be expected. In fact they are usually more or less contrary to the expected result, and seem like mistakes in the economy of nature. For such phenomena he uses the term "unintended." A course or series of events is set on foot generating cer-

[*] *Pure Sociology*, Chap. VII, p. 114.

tain products and properties, when at length some of these latter
begin to work at cross purposes to the general movement and tend
to antagonize it. They were created for one purpose which they serve,
but are found to possess other qualities which develop until they
overshadow the original qualities and react against the normal course
of things.

The Phylogenetic Forces*

ROMANTIC LOVE

Romantic love was due primarily to the greater equality and inde-
pendence of woman. She reacquired to some extent her long-lost
power of selection, and began to apply to men certain tests of fitness.
Romantic love therefore marks the first step toward the resumption
by woman of her natural scepter which she yielded to the superior
physical force of man at the beginning of the androcratic period. It
involves a certain degree of female selection or gyneclexis, and no
longer permitted man to seize but compelled him to sue. But it went
much farther than this. It did not complete a cycle and restore female
selection as it exists in the animal world. It also did away with the
pure male selection that prevailed throughout the androcratic regime.
The great physiological superiority of the new regime cannot be too
strongly emphasized. Its value to the race is incalculable. Female selection, or gyneclexis, as we saw, created a fantastic and extravagant
male efflorescence. Male selection, or andreclexis, produced a female
etiolation, diminutive stature, beauty without utility. Both these un-
natural effects were due to lack of mutuality. Romantic love is mutual.
The selection is done simultaneously by man and woman. It may be
called *ampheclexis*. Its most striking characteristic consists in the
phenomenon called "falling in love." It is not commonly supposed
that this so-called "tender passion" is capable of cold scientific analysis. It is treated as something trivial, and any allusion to it creates a
smile. Yet libraries are filled with books devoted exclusively to it, and
these are as eagerly devoured by philosophers and sages as by school-
girls.

* *Pure Sociology*, Chap. XIV, pp. 396–416.

Such books, of course, are not scientific. They are fictions, romances, lyrics. Yet many of them are classic. Such always contain much truth, and this is almost the only way in which truth of this class is attainable. Serious writers fight shy of the subject. This emphasizes the idea that the subject is not serious. But as it is the most serious of all subjects this naturally creates an almost universal hypocrisy. My favorite way of illustrating this hypocrisy is by contrasting the attitude of society toward a couple, say on the day before and the day after their marriage. To heighten the contrast let us suppose first that one of the two dies on the first of these days. The other is not even a mourner at the funeral. Next that one dies on the latter of these days. The other is then the chief mourner! Yet what real or natural difference is there between the relations of the two on the two days? Evidently none whatever. The only differences in their relations at the two dates are purely artificial and conventional.

Over and over again in the course of our studies into the origin and nature of life, mind, man, and society we have encountered the mysterious but silent power that unconsciously compasses ends not dreamed of by the agents involved, the unheard voice of nature, the unseen hand, the *natura naturans*, the future in the act of being born. But nowhere has there been found a more typical or more instructive example of this than that which is furnished by romantic love. The end is nothing less than perfectionment of the human race. Whatever individuals may desire, the demand of nature is unmistakable. Primarily the object is to put an end to all tendencies toward extremes and one-sided development. It has been said that this mutual selection tends toward mediocrity. This is not strictly true, but there can be no doubt that it tends toward the establishmen of a mean. That mean may be regarded as an ideal. It is not an ideal in the sense of exceptional beauty, unusual size, excessive strength, or any other extraordinary quality. It is an ideal in the sense of a normal development of all qualities, a symmetrical rounding out of the whole physical organism. In this of course certain qualities that are considered most valuable fall considerably below the level attained in certain individuals, and this is why it has been supposed to aim at mediocrity. But it is certainly more important to have a symmetrical race than to have a one-sided, topheavy race, even though some of the overdeveloped qualities are qualities of a high order.

When a man and a woman fall in love it means that the man has qualities that are wanting in the woman which she covets and wishes to transmit to her offspring, and also that the woman has qualities not possessed by the man, but which he regards as better than his own and desires to hand on to posterity. By this is not meant that either the man or the woman is conscious of any of these things. They are both utterly unconscious of them. All they know is that they love each other. Of the reasons why they love each other they are profoundly ignorant. It is almost proverbial that tall men choose short wives, and the union of tall women with short men is only a little less common. Thin men and plump girls fall in love, as do fat men and slender women. Blonds and brunettes rush irresistibly together. But besides these more visible qualities there are numberless invisible ones that the subtle agencies of love alone know how to detect. All such unconscious preferences, often appearing absurd or ridiculous to disinterested spectators, work in the direction of righting up the race and bringing about an ideal mean.[1]

The principle works in the same way on mental and moral qualities, which are at bottom only the expression of internal instead of external differences in the anatomy of the body. For a bright mind is the result of the number and development of the brain cells, and all the manifold differences in character are ultimately based on the different ways in which the brain, the nervous system, and the entire machinery of the body is organized and adjusted. Generally speaking persons of opposite "temperaments," whatever these may be, attract each other, and the effect is a gradual crossing and mutual neutralizing of temperaments. The less pronounced these so-called temperaments the better for the race. They are in the nature of extremes, idiosyncracies, peculiarities, often amounting to intolerable and anti-social caprices, and producing in their exaggerated forms paranoiacs, mattoids, and monomaniacs. Love alone can "find the way" to eliminate these and all other mental, moral, and physical defects.

Romantic love is therefore a great agent in perfecting and balancing

[1] The reverse is of course also true, and a decided aversion between a man and a woman means that their union would result in some prominent defect or imperfection in the offspring. The extent to which the great number of misfits in society, of people who are out of harmony with the social environment, of which criminals only represent the comparatively rare extreme cases, are due to convention and compulsory marriages, which ought never to have been contracted, and which ought to be annulled as soon as they are found to be wrong, is little reflected upon, and society and the church continue to denounce divorces, when the very desire for divorce proves that such marriages are violations of nature and foes of social order and race perfection.

up the human race. It follows as matter of simple logic that it should be given full sway as completely as comports with the safety and stability of society. All attempts to interfere with its natural operation tend to check the progress of perfecting the race. Under the androcratic regime, during which woman had no voice in the selection process, and under the patriarchal system generally where the marrying is done by the patriarch and neither party is consulted, nature's beneficent aims were thwarted, races grew this way and that, and mankind acquired all manner of physical and mental peculiarities. There were of course counteracting influences, and natural love, especially in the middle classes, helped to maintain an equilibrium, but male selection dwarfed woman and slavery dwarfed both sexes. The races of men with all their marked differences have doubtless been in large part due to the want of mutuality in selection for purposes of propagation.

This mutual selection under romantic love can be trusted not to work the extermination of the race from over-fastidiousness. It operates always under the higher law of reproduction at all events. This is proved by the universal influence of propinquity. "Great is Love, and Propinquity is her high priest." If there be but one man and one woman on any given circumscribed area they may be depended upon to love and to procreate. Very bashful persons who shun the opposite sex usually in the end marry the ones with whom circumstances forcibly bring them into more or less prolonged contact. The constant enforced separation of the sexes in the supposed interest of morality causes the sexual natures of those thus cut off from the other sex to become so hypertrophied that there is little chance for selection, and unions, too often illicit, take place with little concern for preferred or complementary qualities. Contrary to the views of moral theorists who advocate such enforced separation, marriages are fewer and occur later in life in societies where the sexes freely commingle and where there is the least restraint. It is also in such societies that the closest discrimination takes place and that the finest types of men are produced.

Where a reasonable degree of freedom of the sexes exists and there is no scarcity of men or of women, this passion of love becomes from a biological, from an anthropological, and from a sociological point of view, the highest of all sanctions. It is the voice of nature commanding in unmistakable tones. . . .

It is a curious fact that there is always a touch of the illicit in all

of the romances of great geniuses—Abelard and Heloise, Dante and
Beatrice, Petrarch and Laura, Tasso and Eleonora, Goethe and Char-
lotte von Stein, Wilhelm von Humboldt and Carlotte Diede, Comte
and Clotilde de Vaux—and the romantic literature of the world has
for one of its chief objects to emphasize the fact that love is a higher
law that will and should prevail over the laws of men and the conven-
tions of society. In this it is in harmony with the teachings of biology
and with those of a sound sociology.

With regard to the essential difference between romantic love and
natural love, it consists chiefly in the fact that the passion is satisfied
by the presence instead of the possession of the one toward whom it
goes out. It seems to consist of a continuous series of ever repeated
nervous thrills which are connected if the object is near, but inter-
rupted and arrested if the object is absent. These thrills, though exceedingly intense, do not have an organic function, but exist, as it
were, for their own sake. That they are physical is obvious, and they
are intensified by various physical acts, such as kissing, embracing,
caressing, etc. In fact it is known that sexuality is not by any means
confined to the organs of sex, but is diffused throughout the body.
Not only are there nerves of sex in many regions, but there is actually
erectile tissue at various points and notably in the lips. Romantic love
gives free rein to all these innocent excitements and finds its full
satisfaction as romantic love in these. Anything beyond this is a return
to natural love, but it is known that such a return is not absolutely
necessary to complete and permanent happiness. This is the great
superiority of romantic love, that it endures while at the same time
remaining intense. It is probably this quality to which Comte alludes
in the passage first introduced into his dedication of the "Positive
Polity" to Clotilde de Vaux, and then put as an epigraph at the head
of the first chapter: "One tires of thinking and even of acting, but
one never tires of loving."

But "true love never runs smooth," and herein lies the chief interest of romantic love for sociology and its main influence on human
progress. Besides its effect thus far pointed out in perfecting the physical organization of man, it has an even greater effect in perfecting his
social organization. The particular dynamic principle upon which it
seizes is that which was described . . . under the name of conation.
It was there shown that the efficiency of this principle is measured
by the distance in both space and time that separates a desire from
its satisfaction. It is the special quality of romantic love to increase

this distance. Under sexual selection proper, or gyneclexis, male de-sire was indeed long separated from its satisfaction, and the interval was filled by intense activities which produced their normal effects according to the Lamarckian law. But these effects, due to male rivalry, were purely biological and only showed themselves in modi-fications in organic structure. They produced secondary sexual char-acters and male efflorescence. This, as we have seen, must have lasted far into the human period. During the long period of androcracy that followed this stage, there was no selection, but only seizure, capture, rape, the subjection, enslavement, and barter of woman. There was no interval between the experience and the satisfaction of desire on the part of men, and very little effort was put forth to obtain women for this purpose. Hence during the whole of this period neither the Lamarckian principle nor the principle of conation could produce any effect. For the great majority of mankind this condition prevailed over the whole world, with greater or less completeness, down to the date of the appearance of romantic love. It still prevails within cer-tain restrictions and under various forms and degrees, in all but the historic races. Under male sexual selection, or andreclexis, so far as its influence extended, there was no interval between desire and satis-faction, no effort, no conation. Its effects were confined to physical modifications, primarily in woman, due to inheritance of the qualities selected by men.

With the advent of romantic love, or ampheclexis, all this was changed. So far as physical modification is concerned the effect was doubled by its application to both sexes alike, and instead of pro-ducing anomalies and monstrosities it worked, as already shown, for equilibration, symmetry, and normal average qualities or ideals. But here we also enter the field of social dynamics, and the principle of conation finds full expression. Schopenhauer has acutely pointed out that the true romance never deals with happiness, only with the troubles, disappointments, labors, and efforts of all kinds in search of happiness. It leads its heroes through a thousand difficulties and dan-gers, and the moment the end is reached the curtain falls! Tarde well says that love is essentially a "rupture of equilibrium." The entire course of a romantic love is a heroic struggle for the restoration of dis-turbed equilibrium. What does all this mean? It means intense activ-ity on the part of great numbers of the human race at the age of great-est efficiency. All this activity is expended upon the immediate en-vironment and every throe of the struggle transforms the environment in some degree. The greater part of this transformation is useful and contributes to its full extent of social progress. In the early days and in the upper classes the demands of woman may have been somewhat trivial. Man must do something heroic, must prove his worthiness by acts of prowess, and such acts may even be opposed to true progress. But they at least develop manhood, courage, honor, and under the code of chivalry they must have a moral element, must defend the right, protect the weak, avenge dishonor, and uphold virtue. But in the lower ranks even then, and everywhere since the fall of the feudal system, woman demanded support and the comforts of life, luxuries where possible, and more and more leisure and accomplishment. To-day she demands a home, social position, ease, and economic freedom. More and more, too, she requires of men that they possess industry, thrift, virtue, honesty, and intelligence. Man must work for all this, and this struggle for excellence, as woman understands that quality, is an extraordinary stimulus, and leads to all forms of achievement.

But man also selects. Romantic love is mutual. Woman has as much to lose as man if it results in failure. And man sets ideals before woman. She must be worthy of him and she gently and naturally bows to his will and follows the course that he gives her to understand is most grateful to him. Thus she develops herself in the direction of his ideals and both are elevated. She may also to some extent transform the environment, if it be no more than the inner circle of the family. The combined effect, even in an individual case, is considerable, and when we remember that in any given community, town, city, state, or country, the majority of men and women pass at least once, sometimes twice or several times, through the phase of life known as being in love, waiting and working for the longed-for day when they are to possess each other, struggling to prepare themselves for each other and for that happy event, we can readily believe that such a stimulus must work great social results. The history of the world is full of great examples, but the volume of achievement thus wrought is made up of thousands, nay, millions of small increments in all lands and all shades and grades of life, building ever higher and broader the coral reef of civilization.

CONJUGAL LOVE

The love of a man for his wife or of a woman for her husband is an entirely different sentiment from that last considered. In a certain way it grows out of it, but it retains none of it, and it has other elements that are wanting in romantic love. Lovers imagine that after marriage they will continue to experience the thrills of love the same as before, the joys of perpetual presence and those of possession added. In this they are certainly mistaken; I will not say disappointed, because, if all is as it should be, what they get is really a far better article than that which they must give in exchange for it. For what, after all, is this beautiful thing called love *par excellence* but a wild, violent, tumultuous passion that completely absorbs their being, excludes all other sentiments and interests, stirs up their inmost depths, and unfits them for the normal pursuits of life? They are incapable while under its spell of enjoying anything else but each the other's presence. The man is unfitted for business, the woman for social life, and both for intellectual pursuits. The only spur that can make either party pursue other things is the sense of doing something that the other desires. It is then done not from any intrinsic interest in the work itself, but from the pleasure of pleasing the other. All the achievement wrought through romantic love, and the quantity is immense, proceeds, at least at first, from this motive, and not from the spontaneous love of work. Its great sociological advantage arises from the fact that this spur impels to activities that without it would never be put forth. Once thus started on the road to achievement an intrinsic interest usually arises and supplements the primary motive.

Romantic love has another drawback, that if anything interrupts it, which constantly happens, joy is turned to grief and even to despair, and so violent is the passion, that these disturbances constantly cause suicide or homicide or both. It is a precarious condition and is never an entirely settled and final state. In other words, it is at best a transient and ephemeral phase, an episode in life, during which it is not felt that this is the end. It is a state of hope, hope for another, an ulterior, a final and settled state to be attained through marriage. Marriage takes place. What follows? The tumultuous billows of romantic love are quickly calmed; the confused and undistinguishable but all-absorbing hopes and fears vanish never to return; the longings, yearnings, cravings of temporary separation disappear; but neither is that leaping, throbbing, exultant joy at meeting any longer felt as such. The prolonged warring of passion is over and peace supervenes. The pair are lovers no longer. James Whitcomb Riley's "Lost Lover" is a "touch of nature," and lovers who marry must say "good-by" as lovers. "Of the old embrace and the kiss I loved there lives no trace."

The philosophy of all this consists in the fact that love is desire and the satisfaction of desire terminates it. All desire is pain, and that love is pain is easily proved by simply imagining it wholly unrequited and unsatisfied. The joy, the pleasure, is not in the love, but in the act of satisfying it, and when that act ceases and satisfaction is fully attained, both the love and the joy, both the pain and the pleasure, end. Of these there remains nothing, and unless something else, something different from either of these, arises to take their place, the soul finds itself in some such a dead calm as vessels experience when they get into the very center of a great storm at sea, where sails and rudders are useless and they can only lie helpless on the bosom of the well and drift at its mercy. There are unphilosophical natures for which this state becomes intolerable. For such there is nothing but the pall of ennui, and, it may be said in passing that this constitutes one of the most common causes of conjugal infelicity. Such natures have accustomed themselves to feed on passion, and when they find passion irretrievably gone they experience sore disappointment and rebel against fate.

But there is a still more unfortunate aspect of the subject. This is a natural consequence of the history of man as we have been tracing it. The romantic and the conjugal sentiments are both derivative and modern. They are the result of different causes and are wholly different. They are so different that both are capable of existing in the same individual at the same time. But they cannot both go out toward the same individual except during the early stages of the latter, where they may be likened to dissolving views. At least, if they do both go out toward the same individual, this is a most happy effect and is highly beneficial to society. I wish to speak here only of those cases, and they are of constant occurrence, in which these two sentiments coexist in the same individual but go out toward different individuals. Moralists are prone to deny the possibility of such a thing, but here, as in many other cases, fiction is more true to nature than social theory, since it is based on social facts. But fiction only gives us more or less idealized illustrations. For the naked facts we must look to social life itself. Here such facts exist in vast numbers and constitute the most difficult problem with which society has to contend.

This obstinate social fact has for its scientific basis a conflict between the biological imperative and the social imperative. The former has been asserting itself during countless ages. The latter has only just come forward in the civilized state of man. Romantic love, as we have seen, as soon as allowed to develop through the emancipation of women, became a powerful aid to the biological imperative in righting up the race that was growing awry under the influence of the extra-normal system which I have called androcracy. The essence of the biological imperative is change, variety, the constant crossing of strains. It is a dynamic principle and works for race vigor and race symmetry. Romantic love favors it and leaves nothing to be desired from this point of view. But that mutual choosing (ampheclexis) of which romantic love consists does not go so far as to claim that unions which it renders advantageous will remain permanently advantageous. Ages of promiscuity that preceded the origin of romantic love left their indelible impress on the race, and but for the counter-principle of conjugal love, monogamy would have been practicably impossible. Those who expect that such a deep-seated race characteristic will wholly disappear in a few centuries of superficial culture find the facts wholly opposed to their ideas. Most of the moralists are utterly ignorant of this real human history, and know no better than to condemn and denounce all manifestations of the biological imperative which do not harmonize with the categorical imperative as taught in their ethical philosophy. But the former principle is infinitely older and far more basic, not to say more reliable as a guide to human conduct.

It is these facts that occasion most of the sexual irregularity in society, and social evils of this class are chiefly due to the failure of men to recognize such fundamental truths, due in turn in the main to their ignorance of the course of human and social evolution, and of the real history of man and society.

Monogamic life, to be successful, requires a certain amount of philosophy. At least it requires character. It calls for qualities of heart and head that lie deep and that come out in their natural purity and vigor as soon as the storm of passion that has kept them in abeyance passes away and permits them to reassert themselves. Then, freed from the thrall of passion, the cleared-up mind can begin to relish other pursuits and gain satisfactions of other and more solid and useful kinds. But in all properly constituted minds there remains at least a memory of the tender emotion which predisposes to the appreciation of mutual companionship not hitherto enjoyed, and this sentiment, planted in natural soil, grows rapidly, and soon begins

to overshadow all others. Herein is found the most typical exempli-
fication of both the kindred principles already alluded to . . . , and
called respectively *propinquity* and *the sanctity of the second person*.
It was shown that one of the happiest traits of human nature consists in the fact that, where there are no repugnant elements, the
mere personal proximity of individuals leads to attachments that
cannot be otherwise explained and have no other basis; to a degree
of appreciation and mutual valuation that is wholly disproportionate
to real worth. But, as in so many other of man's vaunted qualities,
this one goes back far into the animal world:—

> A mastiff dog
> May love a puppy cur for no more reason
> Than that the twain have been tied up together.[2]

Nay, such natural enemies as cats and dogs become fast friends and
affectionate companions when raised together.

Descriptions of conjugal love are hard to find, because, as Schopenhauer says, in all fiction and poetry, where romance ends there ends
the tale, and the marriage, which is the goal of it all, if mentioned at
all, is curtly disposed of in the last line or two that precede the
"FINIS." It is therefore not in fiction that we are to look for a por-
trayal of conjugal love, but rather in works of philosophy, where
attempts are made to find all the social factors. Schopenhauer himself
disposes of it in the following words:—

> However, for the consolation of tender and loving natures, let it be
> added that sometimes to the passion of romantic love [*Geschlechtsliebe*;
> he never recognizes the distinction] there is associated another of wholly
> different origin, viz., true friendship founded on harmony of tempera-
> ment, which, however, for the most part only makes its appearance when
> love proper has been quenched by satisfaction.[3]

Condorcet, who believed in the ultmost freedom of divorce with
a view to the ultimate attainment of the most complete harmony
and mutuality, has pictured this final state of emotional equilibrium
. . . but he does not characterize it as conjugal love. Comte, who
taught that marriage should be indissoluble, essayed on several oc-
casions to portray its perfect state. . . .

There can of course be no doubt that conjugal love is a step more
"psychical" and "spiritual" than romantic love, just as the latter is a

[2] Tennyson, "Queen Mary," Act I, Scene 4.
[3] "Die Welt," etc., Vol. II, pp. 638–639.

step more so than natural love, and in precisely the same sense and
no other, as set forth at the beginning of the last section, and without
implying, any more than in that case, a generic or qualitative distinction. It is in this sense, too, that I have characterized it as "a better
article"—more durable, possessing greater volume, greater utility,
more real worth, and hence more worthy.

Thus far we have assumed only the result of a typical monogamic
union following naturally upon romantic love. It may be said that
such cases, though ideal, are really rare in fact. The widespread existence of conjugal infelicity seems to favor this view, and many deduce
from it the conclusion that "marriage is a failure." But I think the
statistics of marriage from this point of view, could they be obtained,
which they obviously never can be because few are willing to declare
their unhappiness in a public way, would show a slight preponder-
ance of happy over unhappy marriages in enlightened monogamic
countries. The problem of pure sociology is to explain the causes of
unhappy marriages, while that of applied sociology is to show how
they can be removed. With the latter we have here nothing to do. As
to the former I venture to offer the following suggestions:—

It must be obvious that conjugal love as here portrayed cannot
exist under polygamy. It is therefore even more unknown to all the
ages during which polygamy prevailed than is romantic love. It cannot then be older than romantic love and must be confined to the
same races and peoples. The forms of monogamy that preceded that
epoch were chiefly economic in their purpose. They were based on
the conception of natural love and its satisfaction as an economic
commodity, and grew out of the increasing equality in power of
individuals. Polygamy is essentially a monopoly of that commodity,
and as fast as the spirit of liberty gave power to more and more men
in society they revolted against that monopoly and secured as far as
possible an equal distribution of property in women. Owing to the
substantial numerical equality of the sexes this could only be attained
by limiting every man to one wife. Every man who laid claim to more
than one woman deprived another man of his claim to a woman.
Although it is difficult to find any direct announcement of this principle as the basis of monogamy, still it is one of those spontaneous,
self-executing laws that operate silently and perpetually until they
work out the inevitable solution, and the transformed society accepts
the result without knowing why and crystallizes it into an institution
(monogamy), which is first generally accepted, then surrounded with

a legal and religious sanction, and finally defended as something existing in the nature of things or as "ordained of God," or both.

As the property idea gradually disappeared and woman came to be looked upon, not as a possession, a chattel, a slave, but as a human being, a new adjustment became necessary. So long as a wife was only the property of her husband there could be no conjugal infelicity. Between them there existed such a social chasm that no more friction could arise than between a man and his horse. If she displeased him or became recalcitrant she was beaten into submission and shown her place as a simple contributor to his wants and pleasures. But when woman came to be regarded as a human being, if not the equal of man, at least a coagent with man in carrying on the operations of society, all this was changed, and there arose the possibility of a conflict of wills. Both conjugal love and conjugal infelicity are products of mutuality. The recognition of a certain degree of equality is an essential condition to both. The respect and friendly feeling, growing in part out of the memories of requited romantic love and satisfied natural love, as Condorcet has portrayed these sentiments, and in part out of propinquity and the enjoyment of things to which men become accustomed, work upon certain natures in the direction of forming and more and more closely knitting the fibers of conjugal love, and making the parties more and more indispensable and "dear" to each other, until this bond becomes exceedingly close, even indissoluble. On the other hand, the conflict of wills may tend more and more to separate and estrange, and ultimately result either in complete repugnance and separation, or in one or other of the innumerable family jars that make up domestic infelicity. The careful and impartial student will, I think, admit that taking into account the past history and present condition of those peoples among whom romantic and conjugal love exist at all, both sentiments, but especially the latter, are on the increase, and that the human race is growing more and more monogamic. Monogamy involves an enormous moral strain. It is a severe discipline in requiring the constant habit of mutually yielding the one to the other in the exercise of the will. The race is developing in this direction and it becomes from age to age more easy to surrender the will to another with whom everything in life is so closely bound up. There are all degrees of difference in the distance to which different individuals have advanced in this direction, and the present status of marriage simply reflects these differences. To some monogamy is still intolerable, to others it is barely endurable, to still others it is generally satisfactory as the best condition attainable, while to a considerable number it is an ideal condition whose improvement even cannot be conceived of. Finally, as the extreme of development in this line, we have the uxorious, for whom their partners represent perfection, even more complete after marriage than before. Such persons are absolutely blind to all defects, and see each other in an entirely different light from that in which others see them. It is rather common for a man to greatly overestimate even the intellectual powers of his wife. Everybody knows such cases, and we have at least one example among truly eminent men; I refer to the case of John Stuart Mill. Uxoriousness, however, is often one-sided and confined to one of the parties. In such cases it is usually accompanied by more or less jealousy, and often causes unhappiness by restricting the natural liberty of the overrated consort. But uxoriousness is itself a proof of the possibility of ultimately attaining a state of complete monogamy.

All these degrees in the progress of man toward a monogamic state constitute so many examples of the artificial and derivative character of civilization, and show that man is constantly but slowly advancing toward complete sociability. Not naturally social, he is becoming social. If we could imagine uxoriousness to become first mutual and then universal, the problem of marriage would at last be solved. But mutual exaggeration is not desirable, and the perfect state would only be attained by universal mutual attachment coupled with just appreciation.

Conjugal love constitutes a third step in the ethical and esthetic development of the race. We may compare the effects of natural love, romantic love, and conjugal love with the somewhat similar series of steps . . . that were taken by man in the progress of the development of the ontogenetic forces. At each step the sum total of enjoyment is increased and civilization advanced. In the ideal state of conjugal love we seem to reach a condition of felicity, which, so far as it alone can contribute, admits of no improvement. It is full and strong; it is enduring, only ending with life; and it is calm and subdued, so as in no way to interfere with the other normal operations of life.

It remains only to point out that conjugal love is a social force even more efficient than either of the forms of love thus far considered. The principal stimulus is that of providing for the family that naturally grows out of this relation. For the man this is unquestionably the most productive of all stimuli. It is sufficiently intense to cause sustained effort, and instead of being only an episode of a few months' or at most years' duration, it is permanent, and continues from the date of the marriage until death to impel to deeds, if not of glory and renown, at least of usefulness and social value. Instead of having only the incentive of the desire to please another, it has added to this the incentive of work for its own sake. Freed from the distractions arising out of doubt, uncertainty, and the fear of not attaining the great end, he for whom that end is already attained can work for other ends and aim at even worthier ideals. In a word, the mental conditions attending conjugal love are the best possible for human achievement, and, as we have seen, this is the supreme test of social efficiency. Of all the phylogenetic forces, then, conjugal love seems to be the one that has contributed the greatest volume of human achievement, and it is therefore not to be wondered at that it is in the European race and during the past three or four centuries that the greatest achievements have been wrought by man.

MATERNAL LOVE

It is not parental love with which we now have to deal, but with maternal love which is one of those attributes, like natural love, that is commonly, but erroneously, called an "instinct." The intention in using this term is to imply that it is something organic and inherent in the physical constitution, and in so far this view is correct. Maternal love is something that differs *toto coelo* from paternal love and parental affection as distinguished from the maternal emotion. Yet these are constantly confounded by all popular writers, and even philosophers, still dominated by the androcentric world view, usually keep up, and never clear up, the confusion. Thus we find even so close a reasoner as Herbert Spencer saying:—

After this quantitative mental distinction there come the qualitative mental distinctions consequent on the relations of men and women to their children and to one another. Though the parental instinct, which, considered in its essential nature, is a love of the helpless, is common to the two, yet it is obviously not identical in the two. That the particular form of it which responds to infantile helplessness is more dominant in women than in men, cannot be questioned. In man the instinct is not so habitually excited by the very helpless, but has a more generalized relation to all the relatively weak who are dependent upon him.[4]

[4] "Study of Sociology," pp. 374–375.

Now this is, to my mind, a complete confusion of two, or even three, entirely distinct things, viz., maternal love, parental (consanguineal) love, and sympathy. Neither maternal love nor consanguineal love is based on sympathy, or if sympathy enters into them it is as a distinct and added element and has nothing to do with them primarily. Sympathy is the basis of man's moral nature, a product of a high rational power, capable of not only representing to self the painful states of others, but of experiencing the reflex of such representation in self as a form of pain. Maternal and consanguineal love are faculties planted in the nature of man through the laws of survival and advantage as conditions to the preservation and continuance of the race. I wholly reject his theory that they consist essentially or primarily in the love of the helpless. This latter can only be experienced by a highly rational being, while maternal love, at least, is shared alike by man and most of the animals with which most are chiefly familiar.

This last-mentioned fact does not detract from the beauty, purity, or worth of maternal love as a human attribute. It is one of the characteristic attributes of the great class of animals called mammals to which man belongs and is directly connected with the leading function that distinguishes that class from all others, viz., the suckling of the young. The entire mammary system in this great class of animals is a part of the sexual system, and maternal love is primarily a sexual attribute. Thus Dr. Ely Van de Warker remarks:—

Through all the females of the Mammalia there exists a feeling toward their young called the *maternal instinct*. There is no necessity here of going into the question of instinct among animals, as to whether it partakes of the nature of an intellectual process. Whatever be its nature, it is evidently a part of generation, and as such is eminently sexual in its origin.[5]

Here instinct proper is confounded with one of those organic feelings developed in animals for the protection of offspring. This is a much less serious slip than to confound the latter with sympathy, which is often not advantageous at all, was not developed for any such purpose nor in any such way, and is not found in animals except in certain more or less doubtful rudimentary forms.

As the mammary glands are provided with nerves of sexual feeling, these are excited by the suckling of the young, and the mother ex-

[5] *Popular Science Monthly*, Vol. VII, July, 1875, p. 292.

periences a strong sexual pleasure in this act, which in animals must be a valuable motive for permitting it to be done, and thus calculated to preserve the lives of the young. Maternal love is intimately associated with the sexual feeling and grew directly out of it. It is in the mammal therefore that the sentiment of maternal love arose and this sentiment is not only common to all mammals, but is confined to that class of animals. What vague substitutes for it may exist among lower vertebrates is little known, but there may be such. It is probable, however, that the care for young in these classes, including birds, is secured by true instincts, such as those by which eggs are hatched. The principle in the two cases is generically distinct.

The scientific importance as well as the poetic beauty of maternal love is thus portrayed by Haeckel:—

Only in this class [the Mammalia]; is universally found that remarkable mode of caring for the young through the nourishing of the newborn child with the milk of the mother. Herein lies the physiological source of that highest form of maternal love, which has exerted such a momentous influence upon the family life of the various mammals, as well as upon the higher spiritual life of man. Of it truly sings the poet Chamisso:—

> "Nur eine Mutter, die da liebt
> Das Kind, dem sie Nahrung Giebt,
> Nur eine Mutter weiss allein,
> Was lieben heisst und glücklich sein."

If the Madonna is to us the loftiest and purest type of this human mother-love, we see on the other hand in ape-love (*Affenliebe*), in the extraordinary tenderness of the ape-mother, the counterpart of one and the same maternal instinct.

Maternal love is an essentially conservative principle, but such principles are as useful to society as are the active and constructive ones. Hitherto its effects have been chiefly biological in protecting and preserving the race. As a social force it has only operated in a more or less negative way. Sometimes, however, it shows its immense power, and as a human passion it has been made the theme of many tragedies. No author has portrayed this power more accurately or more forcibly than Victor Hugo, and nowhere has he done this better than in his "Quatre vingt Treize" and the rescue of the children from the Tourgue: "Maternity raises no issue: one cannot discuss with it. What makes a mother sublime is that she is a sort of beast. The maternal instinct is divinely animal. The mother is no longer a woman, she is simply female."

And it is true. The highest flights of this passion are those that most assimilate that animal stage when the female was the supreme guardian of her own, the stage of pure gynaecrocracy. Then the female was not only the race, but did all the work of the race and chose the male besides. It was through this long discipline that not only maternal love but maternal courage and maternal efficiency were developed, and notwithstanding the trials to which woman was so long subjected, she is still capable of rising to the occasion, and without hesitation or deliberation, of defending her children in the face of the greatest dangers. Under this powerful spur her acts often seem almost miraculous.

With the advent of a stage of complete equality of the sexes this power is destined, it would seem, to play a much more important role than it has ever done in the past or than it plays in the present state of even the most advanced societies, and if women ultimately become the equals of men in the art of portraying events it is from them that we must expect this passion to be embellished and brought out in the literature of the future.

Consanguineal Love. The love of kindred is probably an exclusively human attribute. It is, however, in all probability, not generically distinct from the consciousness of kind in general, but is such a special form of it that it may be regarded as distinct. It is generically distinct from maternal love, although it is felt by the mother in addition to that sentiment. It is the whole paternal love as such, and also of filial and fraternal love. In the horde there naturally exists a sentiment of attachment on the part of each member of the kinship group for all the rest. Under the matriarchate all consider themselves as brothers and sisters, since the father is unknown, and in all races where there exists uncertainty as to the father, all the members of the clan are brothers.

The social value of this sentiment consists in the fact that it comes to constitute the blood bond, or feeling of attachment that exists among all the members of an ethnic group, and this bond, as is well known, is exceedingly strong. Properly to discuss it, however, it is necessary to look specially at its negative side, since it is here that lies its dynamic quality. In fact, it would have been possible and proper to have treated all the forms of love from their negative or correlative aspects. For to every *love* there is a correlative *hate*, and the force of repulsion is sometimes even more powerful than the force of attraction. The hate corresponding to natural love, romantic love, and conjugal love takes the form of *jealousy*. In the animal world, and to some extent in man, jealousy is a powerful dynamic principle, but its action is chiefly biological. It is the motive to all male rivalry, and it is through this that were developed many of the most striking secondary sexual characters, especially the formidable weapons for fighting, but also strength of frame, muscle, and sinew. But so far as jealousy produces effects upon social structures, they are chiefly destructive, so that jealousy is in the main an antisocial force. . . . The form of hate corresponding to maternal love is quite different. It is mingled with fear, and consists in general hostility to all dangerous or threatening influences. Any person, animal, or thing that stands, or is thought to stand, in that attitude is hated and combated.

When it comes to consanguineal love, especially in that generalized form constituting the blood bond, the corresponding hate becomes *race hatred*. Everybody has some idea of what race hatred means, for it is not confined to savages, but exists between the most civilized peoples. It was at the beginning and has always remained the principal cause of war. To the sociologist it is one of the prime factors of social progress, since without it there could never have been that series of social phenomena . . . resulting, first, in the most important social structures—law, the state, the people, the nation,—and second, in the most important social advances due to the cross fertilization of cultures . . . it is only necessary here to point out their genetic connection with this class of phylogenetic forces, and thus bind all together into a single great group of social phenomena, illustrating the law of sociological generalization.

Biological Origins of
Objective Faculties*

. . . The form of action primarily relied upon by predatory animals is the *ruse*. The creatures preyed upon seek by every means in their

* *Pure Sociology*, Chap. XVII, pp. 483–485, 487–488.

power to escape. Having developed under these conditions they have acquired through natural selection the means of doing this in the majority of cases—fleetness, powers of flight, burrowing instincts, various means of concealment—and if their natural enemies had to depend upon direct pursuit they would usually fail and could not maintain a predatory subsistence. In the means of offense and defense there is a close analogy between nations and animal species. The two have in both cases grown up together. As weapons of war improve so do the forms of armor. It is a perpetual seesaw, but results in more terrible engines on the one hand and more inexpugnable battlements on the other. In the animal world the means of attack and the means of escape have also kept pace, but here the predatory species have not so much relied upon fleetness and strength as upon cunning, not so much upon physical as upon mental qualities. The analogy holds here also, for, as is well known, the victory is not to the strong, but to the inventive nation. Mind in every case is the chief element of strength, and this strength is always proportioned to the degree to which telic methods are employed and the power acquitted to call nature to the aid of muscle and sinew. Notwithstanding the enormous difference between the two planes of telic activity here compared there is absolutely no difference in the principle involved.

The ruse is the simplest form of deception, and this brings out the vital truth that in so far as mind deals with sentient beings deception is its essential nature. It might be supposed that the utilization of psychic forces involved in the deceiving and catching of other living things would require a higher order of intelligence than that required in utilizing physical forces and inanimate objects. Up to a certain point this doubtless is true, and, as we have seen, the first exercise of rational faculty, the primordial tentation and intuition, was in connection with physical environment. But this could only deal with the simplest and most obvious properties and relations, while, as we shall soon see, all other physical phenomena are too obscure to be thus utilized. Paradoxical as it may sound, biotic phenomena and laws are far more simple and intelligible than physical phenomena. . . . The ruse and deception in general do not call for specially high intellectual powers. As Mr. Havelock Ellis says: "The method of attaining results by ruses (common among all the weaker lower animals) is so habitual among women that, as Lombroso and Ferrero remark, in women deception is 'almost physiological.'" [1] And as much might have been said for children, mere babies habitually resorting to it, as every parent knows. It is therefore not surprising that predatory animals, depending for their very existence upon other simple-minded species with specialized means of escape in case of open attack, should soon develop the telic faculty in the particular direction and special form of deceiving and entrapping their prey. Instinct went a long way on this road, as in the spider's toils, and the cunning of the higher animals is so highly specialized and limited that it becomes half instinct.

. . . . .

Deception may almost be called the foundation of business. It is true that if all business men would altogether discard it matters would probably be far better even for them than they are, but taking the human character as it is, it is frankly avowed by business men themselves that no business could succeed for a single year if it were to attempt single-handed and alone to adopt such an innovation. The particular form of deception characteristic of business is called *shrewdness*, and is universally considered proper and upright. There is a sort of code that fixes the limit beyond which this form of deception must not be carried, and those who exceed that limit are looked upon somewhat as is a pugilist who "hits below the belt." But within those limits every one expects every other to suggest the false and suppress the true, while *caveat emptor* is lord of all, and "the devil take the hindmost."

In politics the practice of deception does not differ as much as is generally supposed from that of business. While principle is loudly proclaimed from the stump, interest lies behind it all. Another superficial view is that it is the "politicians" who are making a business of politics and leading the masses to do their bidding. There is only a basis of truth for this but it is not important. Back of the politician and demagogue lie the "vested interests," and these it is that are "making public opinion." It is customary in these days to laud the newspaper, but, except for the little news that it contains, which is to its managers a secondary consideration, the newspaper is an organ of deception.

. . . . .

We might take up the legal profession and we would there find the same general fact—systematic deception. I used to smile when

[1] "Man and Woman," by Havelock Ellis, Third Edition, London, 1902, p. 174.

I heard good and simple country dames say that lawyers lived by lying, and I "studied law," acquitted that profession, and was duly admitted to the bar. But long before the end I had learned that the good country dames were right and I was wrong. I was openly taught by the senior professor that my business was to gain my case, and that I was not to be the judge of the justice of the case. That was matter for the judge. I need scarcely add that I have never pleaded a case.

The form of deception used in warfare is called *strategy*, and the kind that nations practice is known as *diplomacy*. There is collective deception as well as individual deception. There is deception in the home and deception in the church. The average sermon is a more or less clumsy, more or less artful piece of sophistry. A moment's conversation with a stranger will usually reveal the fact that he is trying to deceive you about something, and if you do not discover this it is generally because he has succeeded. Fashionable society consists wholly in sham, quackery reigns in the professions and charlatanism in scientific bodies; falsehood permeates business, and as you look out a car window, the rocks and trees are placarded all over with lies.

3

꩜꩜꩜

The Consequences of Social
Action

Relation of Pure to Applied Sociology *

All this would mean a complete change in the whole method of reform. With the idea of reform has always thus far been associated that of heat rather than light. Reforms are supposed to emanate from the red end of the social spectrum and to be the product of its thermic and not of its luminous rays. But the method of passion and vituperation produces no effect. It is characteristic of the unscientific method to advocate and of the scientific method to investigate. However ardent the desire for reform may be, it can only be satisfied by dispassionate inquiry, and the realization of the warmest sentiments is only possible through the coldest logic. There either is or has been good in everything. No institution is an unmixed evil. Most of those (such as slavery, for example) that many would gladly see abolished entirely, are defended by some. But both the defenders and the assailants of such institutions usually neglect their history and the causes that created them. The hortatory method deals with theses and antitheses, while the scientific method deals with syntheses. Only by the latter method is it possible to arrive at the truth common to both. Only thus can a rational basis be reached for any effective action looking to the amelioration of social conditions.

. . . . .

But applied sociology is not government or politics, nor civic or social reform. It does not itself apply sociological principles; it seeks

* *Applied Sociology*, Chap. I, pp. 5, 9–11.

58

only to show how they may be applied. It is a science, not an art. The most that it claims to do is to lay down certain general principles as guides to social and political action. But in this it must be exceedingly cautious. The principles can consist only of the highest generalizations. They can have only the most general bearing on current events and the popular or burning questions of the hour. The sociologist who undertakes to discuss these, especially to take sides on them, abandons his science and becomes a politician. A large part of Herbert Spencer's writings is of this character. Much of it is to be found even in his Synthetic Philosophy. It only reflects his prejudices and his feelings, and is not scientific. Moreover, as I have repeatedly shown, it is not in harmony with his system as a whole, but rather in conflict with it.

The same may of course be said of nearly the whole social reform movement embraced under the general term "socialism," and including the utopian schools as well as the practical ones—Fourier as well as Karl Marx. They all seek to bring about modifications in social structures. They would change human institutions more or less radically and abruptly. While the advocates themselves do not attempt, except in a few cases on a small scale, to produce these changes, they seek to create a public sentiment in favor of such changes sufficiently general to secure them through legislation. In so far as they actually succeed in this they accomplish their end. The changes are voted or decreed and the state strives to realize them. But often the institutions fail to yield even to the power of the state, and a long struggle follows, such as France is now having with the parochial schools. But all know in how few cases the social reform party acquires political control. This is on account of the stability of social structures. In old settled countries with definite class interests, prescriptive rights, and large vested interests, this is more clearly seen than in new countries, and hence it is in these latter that social reform movements are most successful. But the statistics show that the socialist vote is increasing in all countries where it is made a political issue, and the time may arrive when the party will come into power somewhat generally.

But all this is politics. It is art and not science. The sociologist has no more quarrel with any of these movements than he has with any other political parties,—Whig, Tory, Democrat, Republican. He observes them all, as he does all social phenomena, but they only constitute data for his science. All that he objects to is that any of these things be called sociology. Misarchism, anarchism, and socialism are programs of political action, negative or positive, and belong to the social art. They are not scientific theories or principles and do not belong to social science.

The Efficacy of Effort[*]

Those who take the narrower view and condemn the efforts of society to ameliorate its condition do not content themselves with denying all efficacy in such efforts. This would at least be logical and would compel the advocates of social initiative to prove that such efforts may be successful. But the defenders of *laissez faire* almost uniformly take another step, fatal to their fundamental position, and insist that the interference which they condemn is injurious and pernicious in preventing in some way the successful operation of the benign tendencies of spontaneous natural law. This of course involves the admission of the efficacy of effort, and reduces them to demonstrating that the admitted effects must necessarily be injurious. The main and really difficult task of proving the efficacy of social effort is therefore already performed by the *laissez faire* school. It is not difficult to prove that social effort may have beneficial as well as injurious effects. To have simply maintained the futility, i.e., the complete inefficacy, of social action would have been hardly worth the trouble of condemning it. If it were always wholly without effect and things remained precisely the same after as before, the only rational attitude would be to smile at it as simply wasted effort on the part of deluded people, the same as we smile at the man who spends his whole life in trying to invent perpetual motion. But this has never been the attitude of the *laissez faire* school. They have always condemned social action with warmth and usually denounced it with vehemence as something calculated to do great harm. Indeed, a long list of its mischievous effects has been drawn up and is constantly appealed to. No better arguments could be desired by the defenders of social action. The fact is that the *laissez faire* doctrine is an *ex parte* doctrine. It looks at only one side of a two-sided fact. To a large extent it is arguing without an opponent. Most, though by no means all, of the

* *Applied Sociology*, Chap. II, pp. 14–17.

counts of its indictment are admitted by those who believe in social action. The facts on the other side are almost too familiar to be enumerated and set off against the above-mentioned list. They are far more numerous and important, and their influence for good is immeasurably greater, than the sum total of evil that has resulted from the admittedly frequent mistakes that society has made in its attempts to control social phenomena in its interest. For it is such mistakes that constitute the whole indictment of the *laissez faire* school. I know of no one who has pointed this out or attempted to show as a part of the argument what the beneficial effects of social action have been.

From the great prominence which the individualistic philosophy has assumed, especially in France and England, since the time of the French physiocrats, it is commonly supposed that the general class of ideas upon which it rests has become the prevailing doctrine in these countries and America. There could be no greater mistake than this. While probably the great majority of intelligent persons either avowedly or tacitly subscribe to the doctrine in its main aspects, the fundamental, or as it may be called, subconscious, opinion is everywhere opposed to it. This is proved by the entire history of legislation during that period. The doctrine was undoubtedly salutary at the outset, and it is more or less useful still. It was primarily directed against the pretensions of a class. The action taken by that class can be called social action only in the sense that under all circumstances "the powers that be" actually represent society. That they do so represent it in one sense must be admitted, although, as everybody knows, in view of the general inertia and conservatism of mankind and of the advantage which long tenure and the command of national resources secures to the ruling class, that class may continue in power long after it has ceased to represent society in a more literal sense. The social action against which the new economy was aimed was largely the action of a relatively few individuals. It was egoistic and not social, and had become well-nigh intolerable. The new economy of *laissez faire, laissez passer* was much nearer to the violent revolution in France, in ultimately embodying itself in the state. From the date of this triumph of society over a class, state action in these countries and in all those that have grown out of them has approximated true social action as nearly as could well be expected.

The fundamental error of the modern *laissez faire* school has been that of confounding the present state of the world with the state of the world in the eighteenth century. The civilized world, by whatever name its governments may be called, is virtually democratic, and state action, in the long run at least, is social action in a nearly literal sense.

Now ever since society thus took the reins into its own hands, and far more than during the previous period when it placed them in the hands of a class, it has steadily been taking the initiative, assuming responsibilities, undertaking various enterprises, and taking over into its own control one after another a great array of industries and functions that had hitherto been intrusted to individuals. Economists who have been studying only the political economy of the close of the eighteenth century are alarmed at this, mistaking it for the usurpations of a ruling class, and overlooking the fact that it is true social action. Every step taken in this direction is in response to a public demand. Indeed, society is naturally conservative, and no such step is taken until the demand is practically unanimous and irresistible. The very ones who most strongly call for social action would probably admit the *laissez faire* doctrine in the abstract, but it has no influence on them when it conflicts with interests.

Nor can it be said that all this social initiative has been fruitless. Scarcely a step taken in this direction, from the management of the public finances to the transmission of letters, packages, and messages, has ever been reversed, and the greater part of them have proved so obviously beneficial that they are looked upon as much in the light of social necessities as is the public administration of criminal law, once also left to "private enterprise." What the *laissez faire* economists have done is to go over the long series of these social achievements and cull out a relatively small number of relatively unimportant ones which they declare to have been failures or to be doing harm to society. These are held up as the sufficient proof of the evils of social initiative. Some of them are doubtless failures, and one of the supposed fatal blows against the movement is the number of laws that have actually been repealed, as not accomplishing their purpose. Do not these rather show the wisdom of society in promptly correcting its mistakes when they are found to be such?

A full and candid survey of this field, however, shows that society has always been marching forward in the one irreversible direction, and that its achievements are already multitudinous and of the utmost importance. Social achievement has been the condition to individual achievement, and all forms of achievement are at once the products and the proofs of the efficacy of effort. The "miserable *laissez-faire*" which seeks to check this natural flow of social energy has been appropriately called "moral curae" and "social Nirvana." Over against this doctrine of laissez faire, which is now only a doctrine, stands that of *faire marcher*, which has always been a policy, and without the recognition of which there could be no science of applied sociology.

End or Purpose of Sociology *

PROGRESS VERSUS EVOLUTION

We have already seen that while the subject-matter of pure sociology is achievement, the subject-matter of applied sociology is improvement. The word "progress" is ambiguous. Learned dissertations have been written to prove that the idea of progress, either organic or social, is a purely objective conception and has no reference to the production of more agreeable states of feeling in the beings considered. This is the burden of the argument of Spencer's well-known essay on Progress, its Law and Cause. He says:

Social progress is supposed to consist in the produce of a greater quantity and variety of the articles required for satisfying men's wants; in the increasing security of person and property; in the widening freedom of action enjoyed; whereas, rightly understood, social progress consists in those changes of structure in the social organism which have entailed these consequences. The current conception is a teleological one. The phenomena are contemplated solely as bearing on human happiness. Only those changes are held to constitute progress which directly or indirectly tend to heighten human happiness. And they are thought to constitute progress simply *because* they tend to heighten human happiness. But rightly to understand progress, we must inquire what is the nature of these changes, considered apart from our interests.[1]

He goes on to show that "organic progress consists in a change from the homogeneous to the heterogeneous," and says that "this law

* *Applied Sociology*, Chap. III, pp. 18–28.
[1] Westminster Review, Vol. LVII (N.S., Vol. XI), April 1, 1857, pp. 445–446.

of organic progress is the law of all progress." If this and not the other be the true definition of progress, then applied sociology does not deal with progress. It belongs to pure sociology. In dealing with that branch I have even gone farther than Spencer, and shown that perfection of structure is only a means to the ulterior end of converting the maximum quantity of inorganic into organic matter.[2] It seems to be a question of the proper meaning of the word "progress." I should say that development or evolution would here suit the case better, and social progress may still have as at least one of its definitions the one I gave it in Dynamic Sociology,[3] which is practically that to which Mr. Spencer objected.

It will be seen that Spencer did not deny that structural progress may be attended by an increase in agreeable states of sentient beings including men, but most other writers of his school do very emphatically deny it. It would be easy to fill a volume with citations from Adam Smith, Helvetius, Comte, Schopenhauer, Hartmann, Tolstoi, Durkheim, and others, to the effect that the poor, lowly, and undeveloped classes of society are happier than the rich and intellectually endowed. The "paradox of hedonism," or the formula that to get happiness one must forget it, usually ascribed to John Stuart Mill, but clearly expressed by Kant, belongs to the same class of ideas.

WELTSCHMERZ

The pessimists (Schopenhauer, Hartmann, etc.) deny that there is any remedy for the woes of the world, and as misery increases with social and intellectual development, which they admit to be taking place, the condition of the world will continue to grow worse indefinitely. Some sociologists even incline to that view. Gumplowitz, for example, while admitting the possibility of some amelioration in the condition of mankind in the remote future, thinks that future so remote as to be outside of all practical considerations, like the speculations relative to the ultimate withdrawal of the sun's heat and the secular destruction of all life,—a sort of geological, astronomical, or cosmical speculation about events that may happen millions of years hence.[4] Even this, as private letters from him state, is only his public

[2] Pure Sociology, pp. 113, 114.

[3] Vol. I, p. 67; Vol. II, pp. 161, 174.

[4] Die Wage, V. Jahrgang, Nos. 16 and 18, April 13 and 27, 1902, pp. 248–249, 282–284.

declaration. Esoterically he goes almost as far as Hartmann, but declines to utter his whole thought to the world, for the reason, as he says, that it might do harm, and also because he admits the possibility that he may be wrong,—noble motives, as all must freely confess.

The socialists admit the most that is claimed by the pessimists, but differ from them chiefly in believing that the bad state of things can be remedied by their various specifics. Unfortunately there are many of these, and each school claims that its own particular specific is not only a certain cure but the only cure. It is not probable that any or all of them would have the desired effect if tried, and society does not seem to be ready to give any of them a trial, at least at present. That, however, is no argument against them, and it would be well if a few sincere trials of them could be made to enable scientific sociologists to watch the result. Just as the speculative philosophers tell us that with refinement of physical and mental constitutions the capacity for pain is increased more rapidly than the capacity for pleasure, while the unfavorable social conditions remain the same, so that the pain element constantly gains upon the pleasure element and the world grows worse, so the socialists tell us that the increase of wealth is attended by the increase of poverty; the rich grow richer and the poor poorer, and the number who have diminishes, while the number who have nothing increases, whereby, also, the world grows worse.

I am familiar with all the arguments of both of these classes of people, and I admit the force of them, and while there are many other considerations which greatly diminish the effects ascribed to these causes, and while the case is by no means as bad as it is represented by either class, still it must be candidly admitted to be bad enough, and I can almost agree with Huxley that if there really is no remedy, it would be better if some "kindly comet" could pass by and sweep the entire phantasmagoria out of existence. But while I do not think that any or all of the social panaceas proposed would really remedy the evil, I do not agree with the pessimists that there is no remedy. I deny that society has ever tried to cure itself of the disease called *Weltschmerz*. It has not arrived at that state of self-consciousness at which it has ever seriously considered the question. It is in the same state as a race of animals relative to its true condition. Some savage races are scarcely more advanced. Civilized races are waking up to these purely physical matters. They are in a state of absolute lethargy with regard to social matters. What the human race requires is to be awakened to a realization of its condition. It will then find the remedy for its woes. This must be something more than the feeble plaints of a few individuals. It must amount to complete race consciousness. If this is ever brought about it must be by the same instrumentality that produced all other steps in human progress, viz., science.

ACHIEVEMENT VERSUS IMPROVEMENT

I would never have taken any interest in sociology if I had not conceived that it had this mission. Pure sociology gives mankind the means of self-orientation. It teaches man what he is and how he came to be so. With this information to start with he is in position to consider his future. With a clear comprehension of what constitutes achievement he is able to see what will constitute improvement. The purpose of applied sociology is to harmonize achievement with improvement. If all this achievement which constitutes civilization has really been wrought without producing any improvement in the condition of the human race, it is time that the reason for this was investigated. Applied sociology includes among its main purposes the investigation of this question. The difficulty lies in the fact that achievement is not socialized. The problem therefore is that of the socialization of achievement.

We are told that no scheme for the equalization of men can succeed; that at first it was physical strength that determined the inequalities; that this at length gave way to the power of cunning, and that still later it became intelligence in general that determined the place of individuals in society. This last, it is maintained, is now, in the long run, in the most civilized races and the most enlightened communities, the true reason why some occupy lower and others higher positions in the natural strata of society. This, it is said, is the natural state, and is as it should be. It is moreover affirmed that being natural there is no possibility of altering it. Of course all this falls to the ground on the least analysis. For example, starting from the standpoint of achievement, it would naturally be held that there would be great injustice in robbing those who by their superior wisdom had achieved the great results upon which civilization rests and distributing the natural rewards among inferior persons who had achieved nothing. All would assent to this. And yet this is in fact practically what has been done. The whole history of the world shows that those who have achieved have received no reward. The rewards for their achievement have fallen to persons who have achieved nothing. They have simply for the most part profited by some accident of position in a complex, badly organized society, whereby they have been permitted to claim and appropriate the fruits of the achievement of others. But no one would insist that these fruits should all go to those who had made them possible. The fruits of achievement are incalculable in amount and endure forever. Their authors are few in number and soon pass away. They would be the last to claim an undue share. They work for all mankind and for all time, and all they ask is that all mankind shall forever benefit by their work.

DEFINITION OF JUSTICE

Those who maintain that existing social inequalities are natural and proper and the result of the recognition by society that intelligence, of abilities, or superiority of any kind, deserves to be thus rewarded, are, if they only knew it, going back to natural justice, to the law of the strongest, that prevails in the animal world. The existence of civil justice in human society has already been alluded to as an illustration of the superiority of the artificial over the natural. As its importance is admitted by all, it comes in here as a proof of the inconsistency of all the popular reasoning about social inequalities. After all that has been said about justice, I have never yet seen a statement of the real principle that underlies it, nor a truly philosophical or fundamental definition of justice. The true definition of justice is that it is the enforcement by society of an artificial equality in social conditions which are naturally unequal. By it the strong are forcibly shorn of their power to exploit the weak. The same reasoning which defends existing social inequalities would logically condemn all civil justice. As a matter of fact and of history, the enforcement of justice by society has always been resisted by the strong and denounced as an outrage upon their right to reap the fruits of their superior physical or intellectual power. It is no longer so denounced, at least in the abstract, simply because it has become the fixed and settled policy of all civilized nations. Whenever any institution becomes thus settled it is accepted as a matter of course. It is forgotten that its adoption was the result of a prolonged struggle. The principle underlying it is lost sight of, and other policies involving the same principle are attacked as the first was attacked, the same principle being invoked against them. Thus the claim that the superior intelligence of certain members of society justifies the social inequalities that make up most of the misery of the world does not differ in any respect from the claim of the physically strongest men in a barbaric race to seize and possess the handsomest women and the finest oxen. With the progress of civilization society interfered in this policy and set up in its place what is known as civil, legal, or political justice, which is a reversal of the law of nature and a wholly artificial institution.

THE OLIGOCENTRIC WORLD VIEW

All reasoning on such questions is also always permeated by another vice. It confounds two totally different things. It lays the whole stress on the intellectual aspect and ignores the moral aspect. I use the word "moral" in a somewhat unusual sense, but nevertheless in its true sense, for no word has been so thoroughly perverted as the word "moral." In modern times social inequalities are always looked upon as essentially intellectual inequalities. The words "superior" and "inferior" always mean intellectural superiority and inferiority. The entire philosophy of the present age revolves about these distinctions as their pivot. All science, art, literature, centers on the intellectual. There is an apotheosis of genius, of ability, of talent, of mental brilliancy. So steeped is the public mind in this world view that all who do not display these qualities are wholly lost sight of. The worst is that such only are considered as deserving of anything. All attention is concentrated upon a few exceptions. The effect is to limit the number even of these, because potential ability is given no chance to assert itself. This oligocentric philosophy, which, for the reasons given, has no right to call itself aristocentric, is exceedingly mischievous, and threatens to end in wide intellectual and social demoralization. It is the out-Nietzscheing of Nietzsche.

There is only one science that does not breathe this spirit, and that is sociology. Its point of view is precisely the opposite. It is true that pure sociology takes account of human achievement, but it looks upon it as only a means to the end improvement. All other sciences may be regarded as objective. Sociology is subjective. It recognizes the intellect as the most effective of all agencies, but the intellect was created by the will as a servant of the will, and sociology proposes to hold it to its primary purpose as a means to its primary end,—the well-being of its possessors.

SOCIAL VERSUS POLITICAL JUSTICE

Now the justice of which we have been speaking, vast as its influence has been in securing man's moral advance, is after all only civil and political justice. It is a very different thing from social justice. The civil and political inequalities of men have been fairly well removed by it. Person and property are tolerably safe under its rule. It was a great step in social achievement. But society must take another step in the same direction. It must establish social justice. The present social inequalities exist for the same reason that civil and political inequalities once existed. They can be removed by an extension of the same policy by which the former were removed. The attempt to do this will be attacked and denounced, as was the other, but the principle involved is the same. And after social justice shall have been attained and shall become the settled policy of society, no one will any more dare to question it than to question civil justice.

SOCIAL WELFARE

Let us look more closely into the nature of social justice. The welfare or happiness of mankind consists entirely in the freedom to exercise the natural faculties. The old idea that happiness is a negative state—a state of rest or repose—is completely exploded. It may have grown out of the enslaved and overworked condition of the mass of mankind during such a prolonged period of human history. But everybody knows that a state of inactivity, beyond that needed to recuperate from the effect of previous fatigue, becomes ennui, a state more intolerable than fatigue, which drives the sufferer to some form of activity, no matter what. The physiology of it is that the only source of pleasure is the exercise of some faculty. Conversely, the normal exercise of any faculty is always and necessarily attended with pleasure. Every desire is at bottom the result of some cause that temporarily prevents the normal exercise of a faculty. All want is deprivation, i.e., the withholding of whatever is necessary to set the system into healthy operation. Hunger is the deprivation of the stomach of the food upon which it expends its energy. Love, so long as unsatisfied, is the deprivation of the entire reproduction system of its normal functioning. These are the types of the whole list, and the same is true of all. Taking all the faculties together, physical, mental, spiritual, so far as these can be separated, and their joint normal exercise, is what constitutes happiness, while the deprivation of such normal exercise is what constitutes misery. Complete deprivation would of course be immediately fatal, and the real misery of the world is due to the partial deprivation of the power of men to exercise the faculties by which nature has endowed them. On the other hand, whatever degree of happiness men enjoy is due to the power to exercise their faculties and to no other source.

The problem therefore manifestly is how to secure to the members of society the maximum power of exercising their natural faculties. It is a purely subjective problem and has nothing to do with the relative superiority or inferiority of men. It is wholly independent of the question of their intelligence or ability or social value. It is even independent of their capacity to enjoy or to suffer. It matters not how much satisfaction they are capable of deriving from the exercise of their faculties; it aims only to enable them to enjoy such faculties as they may happen to have.

SOCIAL FREEDOM

From this subjective side the whole upward movement of society has been in the direction of acquiring freedom. If we look over the history of this movement, we shall see that it exhibits three somewhat distinct stages, which may be called in their historical order national freedom, political freedom, and social freedom. The first and prime requisite during the early efforts at nation forming, as set forth in the tenth chapter of Pure Sociology, following upon conquest and subjugation, was the consolidation of the amalgamating group into a national unit capable of withstanding the encroachments and attacks of other outside groups. Until this is attained none of the subsequent steps can be taken. But it involves the elaboration of the crude and antagonistic materials into the only kind of order or organization of which they are capable, viz., the politico-military organization. The salient features of such an organization, as was shown in that chapter, are extreme inequality, caste, slavery, and stern military domination. It is during this state that the industrial system is sketched on the broad lines of social cleavage, resulting in the three great fundamental social tissues,—the ruling class or ectoderm, the proletariat or endoderm, and the business class or mesoderm of the primitive state. These form a strong bulwark and enable the inchoate state to defend itself against hostile elements from without during the subsequent stages in social assimilation. They secure the first great prerequisite, —national freedom.

But individual liberty is at its minimum. The conquered race, which always far outnumbers all other elements, is chiefly in bondage, and the struggle for political freedom begins. Ultimately, as the history of the world shows, this is in large measure attained. Throughout antiquity, the Middle Ages, and down to the middle of the nineteenth century, this was the great, all-absorbing issue. One after another the bulwarks of oppression—slavery, serfdom, feudalism, despotism, monarchy in its true sense, nobility and priestly rule—fell; the middle or business class, otherwise called *bourgeoisie* and third estate, gained the ascendant, which it still holds, and political freedom was attained.

So all important did this issue seem that throughout the eighteenth century and down to near our own time it was confidently believed that, with the overthrow of political oppression and the attainment of political freedom, the world would enter upon the great millennium of universal prosperity, well-being, and happiness. But this was far from being the case. As sages predicted, events have proved that there remains another step to be taken. Another stage must be reached before any considerable degree of the hopes that were entertained can be realized. This state is that of *social freedom*. The world is today in the throes of this third struggle. Military and royal oppression have been overthrown. Slavery, serfdom, feudalism, have disappeared. The power of the nobility and the priesthood has been broken. The civilized world is democratic, no matter by what name its governments are called. The people rule themselves by their sovereign votes. And yet never in the history of the world was there manifested greater unrest or greater dissatisfaction with the state of things. National freedom and political freedom have been achieved. Social freedom remains to be achieved.

But the problem of social freedom is much more difficult and subtle than either of the others. It was a comparatively simple matter to deal with the state and the ruling class. These were always conspicuous and locally circumscribed. The forces that prevent social freedom, on the contrary, are hidden and universally diffused through the social fabric. They give rise to questions so recondite and obscure that the clearest thinkers differ as to their solution. These questions cannot come into the political arena until there is a certain harmony or consensus of opinion concerning them. In short, they are the proper subjects of scientific investigation. The only science that can deal with them is sociology. Their study and solution belong to applied sociology.

Truth and Error*

ERROR

As the religious ideas thus far considered consist entirely of error, there being no objective truth corresponding to spiritual beings, and as religious structures are based directly and exclusively upon religious ideas, if the latter really served the useful purpose above described, it seems to follow that error may be useful. This may be a shock to some minds, but it serves to show the futility of most abstract theories, such as that truth is always necessarily useful and error necessarily injurious. Until we rid ourselves of these and are content to rest our case upon observed facts, we have no real standing in court. What the course of human evolution would have been had there been no religious ideas and no religious structures, it is perhaps idle to speculate, because there are no facts to support any theory, the existence of both being, as we have seen, a necessity in the nature of things. We cannot even conceive of the development of a race of rational beings in a world like ours without having to pass through the whole religious stage as described.

Religious ideas and structures are an exclusively rational condition. The whole animal world is without either. Animals, including the prehuman ancestor of man, are as completely devoid of all knowledge

* *Applied Sociology*, Chap. VI, pp. 65–80, 80–82.

of the laws and principles of nature as was the most primitive human being, or, if possible, more so. But this is only ignorance; it is not error. Error is a pure product of reason. It arises from an effort on the part of a rational being to interpret phenomena. It consists in a false interpretation of phenomena due to insufficient knowledge. It could not be avoided because appearances in nature are always different from the reality and usually nearly or quite the opposite of it. . . . It is absolutely impossible for a race of beings to emerge out of the non-rational and pass into the rational state without accumulating a vast load of error.

That reasoning from inadequate data is always misleading has been seen by the greatest logicians. . . .

. . . . .

CONSEQUENCES OF ERROR

Only a brief and partial enumeration of the consequences of the universal belief in spiritual beings can be attempted here, but in most cases they are already so familiar to all well-read persons that a mere mention of them is sufficient. The important point is to show that the greater part of the evils from which the human race has suffered, evils unknown to animal races, are really due to error, i.e., to false conclusions drawn from inadequate premises. The most shocking of all these consequences unquestionably is the widespread custom of sacrificing human victims at the funerals of chieftains. . . .

A survey of this field shows that this horrid practice is comparatively rare among the very lowest races, and reaches its maximum in races quite well advanced toward or fairly into the status called barbarism. . . .

. . . . .

. . . . It really took place in consequence of that advanced state, i.e., in consequence of the fully developed reasoning powers of that people, by means of which they were capable of elaborating a systematic doctrine relative to the spirits of the dead. This body of doctrine is crystallized into a universal belief that these spirits exist and will follow their master into the next world and there minister to his wants. As Spencer says:

The intensity of the faith prompting such customs, we shall the better conceive on finding proof that the victims are often willing, and occasionally anxious, to die. . . . Garcilasso says that a dead Ynca's wives "vol-

unteered to be killed, and their number was often such that the officers
were obliged to interfere, saying that enough had gone at present." [1]

This belief is a typical world view. It is universal not only in the
sense that it exists in all human races at the proper stage in the development of the rational faculty, but also in the sense that it is shared
by every member of the group without exception. Some one has well
said that there are no dissenters among savages. Comte has been criti-
cized for saying that fetishism represents "the most intense theological state," [2] but it is perfectly true from our present point of view,
which is that from which Comte viewed it, as the context shows. Such
ideas are an integral part of the mental existence of a people; they
permeate the society and sway the entire mass. Every act, public or
private, is determined by them, and no act is too shocking or terrible
to be shrunk from if dictated by the logic of the dominant idea.

The practice of placing the belongings of a dead person in his grave
for his use in the next world is a simple corollary from the general
reasoning of primitive peoples relative to the nature of the soul. Like
everything else in savage life, it was carried to the greatest extremes
and ultimately resulted in some tribes in an enormous destruction of
property. . . . It is in fact a more serious evil than the sacrifice of
human victims, because it is practised by persons of all classes, whereas
sacrifices are mainly confined to royal funerals. In many cases all that
man has is either buried with him or destroyed in one way or another,
it often being regarded as sacrilegious to make any further use of a
man's property after he has passed away. This practice also lasted
much longer in the history of the mental development of a people
than that of sacrificing. Long after the latter has been discontinued
the former is kept up, partly as a substitute, and we find it persisting
among half-civilized peoples down almost to our own time. In some
parts of China, for example, a wealthy family is sometimes completely
ruined by a costly funeral. Indeed, the funerals among civilized peoples are often extravagantly expensive, and this waste of property may
be regarded as a survival of the barbaric practice of burying or destroying all the property of a dead person.

Another direction which this same class of primitive logic took was
that of the erection of costly tombs for the remains of great warriors
and rulers. This has also been an almost universal practice, and one

---

[1] Spencer, Principles of Sociology, Vol. I, p. 205, Section 104.
[2] Philosophie positive, Vol. V, p. 39.

that extended far down into the latest stages of barbarism. These tombs are scattered all over the world and are often about all that remains of an extinct civilization. An enormous amount of labor has been expended upon them,—labor thus withdrawn from productive industry and of course involving a corresponding amount of misery among the people. The pyramids of Egypt represent the highest point to which this practice was ever carried, for they are neither more nor less than the tombs of the great kings of that country. Those who visit them are usually profoundly impressed with them as achievements of human art at so early a period, and rarely reflect upon their significance from the economic and sociological standpoint. There has been, however, one exception to this in the case of Mr. Herbert Spencer, who, as we might expect of him, reflected upon the conditions that could have brought such remarkable objects into existence. In his autobiography he describes his visit to them, and says:

With the one memorial is associated the name of Cheops, or, as he is now called, Shufu or Koofoo—a king who, if we may believe Herodotus, kept a hundred thousand men at work for twenty years building his tomb; and who, whether these figures are or are not correct, must have imposed forced labor on enormous numbers of men for periods during which tens of thousands had to bear great pains, and thousands upon thousands died of their sufferings. If the amounts of misery and mortality inflicted are used as measures, this king, held in such detestation by later generations that statues of him were defaced by them, ought to be numbered among the few most accursed of men.[3]

Under the head of Consequences of Error I had planned to treat in this work somewhat at length some dozen other illustrations, for all of which I have been collecting materials for many years; but I realize that this would unduly expand this chapter, while most of the data are accessible to the reading public, and I have decided that it will be sufficient simply to enumerate the principal heads. This I shall do in something like the order in which the practices occur in the course of the general development of the reasoning powers and intelligence of mankind. This chronological order is also the logical order; but I would not wish to imply that it relates to historical chronology, but simply to the successive stages attained by peoples, irrespective of the absolute times at which such stages were reached. Comte has been severely attacked by persons who, if they had read his works

[3] An Autobiography. By Herbert Spencer, New York, 1904, Vol. II, pp. 403–404.

at all, had read them carelessly, and who accused him of maintaining that the "three stages" followed one another in strict chronological order. He made no such claims, and repeatedly explained that two or more of the great leading world conceptions always coexisted, not only in different parts of the world but also among the same people and even in the same mind. In all such discussions it is necessary to abstract the conditions or states of mind and consider them by themselves and independent of dates and other human events. In the following enumeration this is all that is meant by the order in which the practices or customs are arranged.

1. *Self-mutilation.* This is a wide-spread custom, performed chiefly at funerals, or often prolonged for days as a token of grief, and believed in some way to please the departed spirit or appease angry gods. It takes a variety of forms, but usually consists in the mourners cutting and gashing themselves with whatever sharp instruments they may possess.

2. *Superstition.* This term is much too general for convenient use. It really embraces all the forms of error that have been or are to be enumerated. But by its use here it is meant to group under it a great mass of customs and practices which do not usually involve the destruction of human life, but which have for their principal effect to restrict the liberty of action and fill the minds of men with a thousand ungrounded fears and terrors. It also serves as an effective bar to all intellectual or material progress, and as it continues on through all the stages of barbarism into that of civilization, this latter aspect becomes more serious. As an example may be mentioned the fact, alleged at least, and probably real, that the chief objection to the construction of railroads in China was that the noise and jar of the trains would disturb the dead.

3. *Asceticism.* This is unknown in savagery and is scarcely possible in any stage of true barbarism. It was reserved for a high state of intellectual development, but it is based, as truly as human sacrifice, upon the belief in spiritual beings and a future spiritual existence. Though based like the rest mainly on fear, it contains an element of hope. As Sir Thomas More admitted, the real end sought by it is pleasure to self,[4] and Hartmann declares that it is thoroughly egoistic.[5] The horrible self-tortures that have been practised by thousands of people in all ages under this delusion have been vividly portrayed, and

[4] Utopia (1516). Murray's English reprints, London, 1869, No. 14, p. 116.
[5] Philosophie des Unbewussten, Bd. II, pp. 366, 373.

it would be easy to fill a volume with their recital. The milder forms that have long prevailed in the leading civilized countries, called puritanism in America, are dangerous to health and destructive of happiness and of progress.

4. *Zoolatry.* Animal totemism among savage and barbarous tribes, which is itself a form of animal-worship, but is comparatively harmless, becomes a serious matter when in more civilized peoples like those of India it makes vermin, serpents, and dangerous wild beasts sacred and interdicts their destruction. The logic of these practices grows out of the belief in the transmigration of souls through the bodies of these animals into those of man and back from men to animals. Reference was made to this in Dynamic Sociology (Vol. II, p. 271), but it still continues, and the high rewards offered by the British government seem scarcely to tempt the superstitious natives of that country. Statistics of mortality from these sources are annually collected, but they must fall far short of the true figures. In 1899, 24,621 persons died in India from snake bite alone, while in 1901 the number was 23,166. Tigers, leopards, bears, wolves, and hyenas destroy between 2000 and 3000 more each year. The cobra, the tiger, the leopard, and other dangerous snakes and animals are sacred and occupied by the souls of men.

5. *Witchcraft.* The belief in the power of certain persons to project their spirits into other persons to project their spirits into other persons and "possess" them is almost universal among all but the most enlightened peoples. Some form of sorcery is believed to be practised by all savage and barbaric races. Both sexes have this power, but the tendency was to limit it more and more to women. In the Middle Ages it took the form of witchcraft and lasted until into the eighteenth century. Indeed, it is not over now, and is still practised in Mexico, a witch having been burned at Camargo in 1860. A suit was brought in 1902 at Chicago against a woman for bewitching another and causing her hair to fall out.[6] Witchcraft was fully believed in by Luther, Melanchthon, John Wesley, and Lafitau, and was declared to be a fact by Blackstone.[7] It is now completely discountenanced by all enlightened persons regardless of their creed, and they all agree that there never was any such thing as the bewitching of one person by another. The thousands of witches who have been put to death, often burned at the stake or horribly tortured, must

[6] See the newspapers of about July 29, 1902.

[7] Commentaries, Book IV, p. 60.

therefore have all been innocent victims of this hideous error that seized and held fast the minds of men through so many centuries. One would suppose that a fact like this would cause everybody to doubt every opinion held without the most convincing proof, but in the face of it the world still clings to hundreds of scarcely less absurd ideas, though most of them are incapable of leading to such shocking consequences.

6. *Persecution.* I confine this for the present to religious persecution, i.e., to the persecution of so-called heretics. A heretic is a person who has a somewhat, often only slightly, different religious belief from a larger body of persons in the country in which he lives, and who have acquired power over the lives and liberties of citizens. This is confined to what are called civilized countries, because, as we have just seen, there are no differences in the belief of savages. A difference of belief is a mark of civilization; and it has always happened that the dissenters were the more civilized. Their persecution, therefore, and wholesale destruction, as in the case of the Inquisition, means the slaughter of the *elite* of mankind. Those who can escape fly to other lands, and the persecuting country is emasculated of all its vigorous and virile elements. The object is to make belief absolutely uniform, i.e., to reduce a civilized people to the condition of a savage people. This has been repeatedly done, notably in Spain, and history has recorded the consequences. A people that tolerates no differences of opinion is degenerate and must take a second or lower place.

7. *Resistance to truth.* More serious probably for mankind at large than any other one of the consequences of error, or perhaps than all of them combined, is the opposition that error always offers to the advance of truth. In the earliest stages there was no possibility for the truth to emerge at all from the mass of error. The error was accepted by all without any single one ever so much as thinking of questioning it. All the steps toward truth were taken at later stages, chiefly in peoples that ethnologists class as civilized. Every heresy, however slightly the belief may differ from the dominant or orthodox belief, is a step toward the truth, a greater or less reduction in the amount of error in the belief. Persecution for heresy, therefore, which was considered under the last head, was the last form that resistance to truth assumed. The present head is meant to include other forms, most of which involved persecution, but some of which were somewhat independent of persons. The most of them may be included under the general designation of opposition to science.

We saw that the whole mass of primitive error was the result of a false interpretation of natural phenomena. The true interpretation of the same phenomena was the work of thousands of patient investigators continued through centuries, and was usually practically the reverse of the prevailing false interpretation. Thus shadows and reflections were found to be due to the nature of light and the laws of radiation after the science of optics had been founded; echoes were explained on the now familiar principles of acoustics; dreams, delirium, insanity, epilepsy, trance, and even death are explainable on natural principles contained in the sciences of psychology, physiology, pathology, and psychiatry; and although many things are still obscure in relation to them no specialist in any of those sciences ever thinks of calling in the aid of indwelling spirits to account for any of the facts.

All the anthropomorphic ideas upon which primitive error rests are dispelled by science. Astronomy has taught the nature of the heavenly bodies and the laws of their motions. Air is understood and is nothing like the primitive idea of spirit but is a mixture of gases in nearly uniform proportions. Lightning is as well understood as are any of the manifestations of electricity. And so with the whole series of physical phenomena upon which primitive man built his superstructure of life, will and intelligence in inorganic nature.

All this truth that science revealed had to struggle against the dense mass of primitive error which it was destined to overthrow, and the resistance was enormous. The discoverers of truth have been the victims of all forms of persecution, and the truth revealed has been formally condemned and anathematized. Truth has never been welcome, and its utterance was for ages fraught with personal danger. Fontenelle advised those who possessed new truths to hold on to them, because the world would only punish them for their utterance. Nearly everybody acted upon this principle, and either refrained from investigating or from promulgating new ideas. Descartes wrote his Traite du Monde, but suppressed it for these reasons.[8] The chief effect was that of deterring talented men from trying to discover truth, and the greater part of all intellectual energy has been diverted into safer but comparatively useless channels.

The history of the later phases of this opposition to the progress of science has been so ably presented by numerous writers that it would be superfluous to enter into it here, even if space would permit. I

[8] Œuvres de Descartes, Paris, 1844, pp. 38, 47.

scarcely need draw special attention to the contributions of two Americans to this subject, so familiar are their works.[9]

This opposition to science may be supposed to have some value in rendering it necessary that the discoverers of truth assure themselves beyond a peradventure of the correctness of their position before venturing to promulgate their ideas. Some have partially excused it on this ground. But for this to be true it would be necessary to suppose that anything that was absolutely demonstrated would be accepted. This has never been the case. There has never been any attempt to verify discovery. The opposition has always been dogmatic. It cannot be true because opposed to the current world view. No amount of demonstration would avail. Those who believe things because they are impossible are not going to believe anything because it is proved.

But there is no need of this kind of illegitimate opposition to the discovery of truth. There is always an abundance of legitimate opposition to it. This was shown in Pure Sociology under the head of "How Science Advances." [10] There is no danger of any error in science gaining a permanent foothold. Every proposition is immediately doubted and attacked, but it is attacked with the legitimate weapons of scientific experimentation and not with the rack and thumb-screw. In other words, it is reinvestigated by others and either confirmed or rejected. Usually a part is confirmed and part rejected, but at any rate the opposition is always compelled to admit all that is true and the original discoverer is compelled to abandon all that is not true. The difference is the amount of established truth contained in the discovery. In the kind of opposition to science that we have been considering it is all loss and no gain.

8. *Obscurantism.* This is another form of persecution, only a little more subtle than the form last considered. Indeed, it is only a case of this latter, and might have been treated under the general head of resistance to truth. But by it is meant certain refined phases of this resistance practised by nations claiming to be civilized. Its principal method consists in the prohibition or suppression of books and writings and the general censorship of the press. This has been chiefly practised by the Christian church, both the Catholic Church and the

[9] History of the Conflict between Religion and Science, by John William Draper, fifth edition, New York, 1875 (International Scientific Series, No. 12). A History of the Warfare of Science with Theology in Christendom, by Andrew Dickson White, in two volumes, New York, 1897.
[10] Pages 8–12.

Greek Church. It is still practised by both these churches, but so far as the former is concerned it is now chiefly a matter *pour rire*. Still, within the church itself it is somewhat effective. With the Greek Church it is more serious because sanctioned by the government of the nation of which that is the state church. But for several centuries it was effective in the Catholic Church, and most of the progressive literature of that period was rendered inaccessible to the general public. For it is with books as with men; those that dissent from the current world views are the ones that contain truth. As Helvetius said in a book that he refused to publish during his lifetime, "it is only in the prohibited books that the truth is found." [11]

It is interesting to glance over the Papal Index Librorum Prohibitorum. There are to be found the majority of the works that the world recognizes as great or epoch-making. This Index continues to be issued periodically, and I have recently amused myself in scanning the pages of the latest volume. The Russian government publishes a similar Index. One of its numbers has lately appeared containing the books condemned between 1872 and 1891. It contains works by Herbert Spencer, Ernst Haeckel, Lecky, Zola, Ribot, etc.[12] The prohibition is made effective by not allowing Russian translations to appear at all. The great mass of the people are thus effectually prevented from ever reading a book. I have never doubted that many of the books condemned by the Russian censors were so treated on account of other than religious sentiments contained in them. If it is feared that they may tend to render the people discontented with their lot or dissatisfied with the government, it is easy to find passages that can be objected to on religious grounds, and to allege these as the reasons for prohibiting a work. In the light of prevailing political opinion ministers would scarcely dare to assign political reasons. This was attempted in Germany at the time of the publication of Frederick's diary with rather unsatisfactory results. The numbers of the Deutsche Rundschau containing the article came to America with the pages cut out. I went to a bookstore and bought for ten cents a small

[11] (Quotation in French) (De l'Homme, etc., London, 1773, Vol. I, pp. iv, 6. Cf. p. 62.)

[12] I am indebted to Mr. George Kennan for these facts, he having obtained a copy of the work. He informs me that Dynamic Sociology is No. 86 in the list, and that the reason assigned is as follows: "Condemned and publication forbidden by the Committee Ministers, March 26, 1891 [Old Style]. The book is saturated with the rankest materialism." The reader may remember the account given in the preface to the second edition of the seizure of the Russian translation.

duodecimo pamphlet containing the English translation. Probably thousands read it that never would have done so if it had not been prohibited, at least in other countries than Germany. In a free country any such attempt at obscurantism is in the nature of an advertisement and it is to be hoped that the time will soon come when it will be no longer possible to dam up the stream of truth.

Nevertheless, in the darker ages of the world, and still at present, in the darker lands, where political liberty has not yet been achieved, it cannot be doubted that human progress has been and is being greatly retarded by cutting off the light and not allowing it to penetrate into places where it would be seen and welcomed if it could be admitted. There are certain forms of falsehood which are justified on grounds not widely different from the jesuitical doctrine that the end sanctifies the means. There is an old proverb which in its French form says: *Calomniez, il en restera toujours quelque chose.*[13] It is a kind of obscurantism. A slander or a falsehood, as Oliver Wendell Holmes said, "makes a great deal of leeway in proportion to its headway." The official reports of the Russian generals in the war that has just been waged between Japan and Russia seemed to embody the proverb above quoted. The bad news was not given out. The driving in of pickets preceding the battle was loudly proclaimed as a Russian victory, but the defeat that followed was suppressed and the world did not learn the truth until the Japanese generals were ready to make their report. This could always be depended upon, never exaggerating the gains and often seeming to exaggerate the losses. On the Russian reports no dependence whatever could be placed.

This enumeration of the consequences of error growing out of religious ideas might of course be greatly prolonged, but the examples given are sufficient to indicate its character. There are, however, other consequences of error which do not come exactly under this head, but which are often equally serious. They consist of erroneous world views which cannot be directly, or at least can only be partially, ascribed to the belief in spiritual beings. Among these I would put first, as having exerted the most baneful influence on the human race, that which I have described in Pure Sociology as the Androcentric World View. It is not so much the terrible sufferings that womankind has had to endure in consequence of this gigantic error as it is the dwarfing and stunting influence that it has exerted throughout such a prolonged

[13] For a full history of this proverb, see King's Classical and Foreign Quotations, third edition, London, 1904, No. 241, p. 33.

period. We can scarcely form any idea of what the human race would have been if a true and just conception of both man and woman had always prevailed. And as this false world view still prevails so universally as to render it a veritable world view still even to-day, we can realize that there is something for applied sociology to do.

As growing directly out of the Androcentric World View and the institutions founded upon it may be mentioned the prevailing error with regard to motherhood. The bringing of a new human being into the world is universally recognized as among the noblest and holiest of duties, but there is the proviso which is agreed to with equal unanimity that unless it takes place under the sanction of civil or ecclesiastical law it is not a duty but a crime, to be punished with the severest penalties that society can devise. The amount of misery that this false theory of life entails upon humanity is beyond all calculation. A young woman has a child outside of wedlock; it may have been the consequence of love as pure as ever animated the human breast. She is disgraced and drowns her offspring in a pool. The maternal instinct haunts her, and she goes back and frantically recovers and embraces the body of her dead child. The officers of the law discover her and she is seized, imprisoned, tried, condemned, and hung.[14] What a series of horrors growing out of the most innocent, natural, and noble of all human actions! All due to a false world view, to a great human error hanging over the civilized world.

. . . . .

TRUTH

Mr. Robert G. Ingersoll, when asked if he could suggest any way by which, if he had the power, he could improve the universe, replied that he would first make health "catching" instead of disease. All this error of which we have been speaking may be looked upon as so much social disease, which, under the laws of imitation so ably worked out by M. Tarde, is contagious, and is passed on from mind to mind and from age to age. And just as the mission of medical science is to do away with disease and replace it by health, so the mission of social science is to do away with error and replace it by truth. It may be said that this is the mission of all science, and so it is. But all the science

[14] This assumed case has been nearly paralleled by a recorded fact. See J. Novicow, L'Affranchissement de la femme, Paris, 1903, p. 1.

in the world has failed to remove any of the great world errors. They still stand in the face of it and are shared by the mass of mankind. The false ideas have, indeed, been disproved, and the true explanation of natural phenomena have been furnished, but all this has little social value. The number who know the truth is relatively insignificant even in the most enlightened countries. The business world takes up the scientific discoveries and utilizes them, and the mass avail themselves of the resultant advantages, but they have no idea of the true significance of scientific discovery. The great bulk of every population on the globe is steeped in error. A wholly emancipated person finds himself almost completely alone in the world. There is not one perhaps in a whole city in which he lives with whom he can converse five minutes, because the moment any one begins to talk he reveals the fact that his mind is a bundle of errors, of false conceits, of superstitions, and of prejudices that render him utterly uninteresting. The great majority are running off after some popular fad. Of course the most have already abrogated their reasoning powers entirely by accepting some creed. The few that have begun to doubt their creed are looking for another. They may think they are progressing, but their credulity is as complete as ever, and they are utterly devoid of any knowledge by which to test the credibility of their beliefs. And yet these may be what pass for "educated" persons, for, as a matter of fact, the education that is afforded by the systems of the world not only does not furnish any knowledge but expressly disclaims doing this, and aims only to "draw out" some supposed inherent powers or talents. But, as we have already seen, these native powers, deprived of all the materials upon which to exert themselves, are not merely useless but are in a high degree dangerous and pernicious. Ignorance is comparatively safe. It is error that does the mischief, and the stronger the reasoning faculties working upon meager materials the more misleading and disastrous the erroneous conclusions thus drawn are for mankind.

Of course the great desideratum is to supply the data for thinking, and to supply them to all mankind and not merely to a handful of the elite, but the problem is how to do this. Truth is unattractive. Error charms. It holds out all manner of false hopes. It is a siren song that lures frail mariners upon desert isles, where with nothing to nourish the soul they perish and leave their bones to bleach upon the barren strand. All the shores of the great ocean of time are strewn with these whitened skeletons of misguided thought. Truth furnishes the only real hope. It is truth that should be made attractive, alluring, contagious, to such a degree that it shall penetrate the whole mass of mankind, crowding out and replacing the error that now fills the world.

Social Appropriations of Truth*

The idea of causation which it is necessary to entertain in order to secure progressive action on the part of man is first, that the cause of any phenomenon is a true cause, and second, that it is an adequate cause. A true cause is an efficient cause. It is a force, and force must be conceived as impact or as pressure. If the wind tears the branches from trees, unroofs houses, or fills the sails of vessels, it must be realized that air is a material substance that is set in violent motion by meteorological conditions and acts directly upon other substances producing the observed effects. If we cannot see this so plainly in the forces of heat, light, electricity, and gravitation, our faith in them as true forces must not be diminished thereby. This does not preclude us from speculating as to the true nature of these subtle agencies, only it must not carry us so far as to invest them with supernatural attributes. We may even go so far as to maintain that matter is spirit, but in the sense that it is endowed with intelligence and will, and can and does take that form when organized in the appointed way and to the required degree. But will and intelligence themselves are subject to law and are in fact as rigidly determined as are the winds or the electric currents.

With regard to the adequacy of causes, I cannot better illustrate it than by a personal experience. When [I was] collecting around Fish Lake, Utah, in the Wasatch Range in 1875, a party of Pai-Ute Indians were encamped at the outlet of the lake. The chief was sick, and supposing me to be a "medicine-man," they appealed to me to cure him. I promised to send him some medicine, gathered some of the juniper berries abundant there, roasted and pulverized them, put the powder in a cap box and sent it to the chief, knowing that it would be practically inert and certainly harmless. It was returned from fear that it

* Applied Sociology, Chap. VII, pp. 89–90, 95–101.

might be poison. I told the messenger that I would throw it into the lake. The next morning the Indian camp was in an uproar from fear that I had thrown the medicine into the lake and poisoned all the water of the lake. Fortunately I had not yet destroyed it, and calmed their fears by letting them see me burn it up in the camp-fire. This little incident showed that those Indians had no conception of the quantitative relations of cause and effect. A single gram of poison in a whole lake would have alarmed them as much as the half-ounce that I had prepared. I have often met people that showed the same inability to see that quantity had any relation to effect in the matter of poisons. This is very largely true in other matters in undisciplined minds, and a large part of the error and consequent misguided action of mankind is the result of a lack of power to perceive the inadequacy of many causes to produce the effects ascribed to them. The world must learn not only to distinguish a true from a false cause but also to judge of the adequacy of a cause to produce an effect.

. . . . .

INTELLECTUAL EGALITARIANISM

The proposition that the lower classes of society are the intellectual equals of the upper classes will probably shock most minds. At least it will be almost unanimously rejected as altogether false. Yet I do not hesitate to maintain and defend it as an abstract proposition. But of course we must understand what is meant by intellectual equality. I have taken some pains to show that the difference in the intelligence of the two classes is immense. What I insist upon is that this difference in intelligence is not due to any difference in intellect. It is due entirely to difference in mental equipment. It is chiefly due to difference in knowledge, if we include in knowledge a familiarity with the tools of the mind and an acquired ability to utilize the products of human achievement. . . . Each age of the world's history stands on a platform erected by all past ages. It is true that all teh members of society have the use to a certain extent of the products of past achievement, but in no sense do those members stand on the elevated platform who do not actually possess the heritage of the past. Now, as a matter of fact, it is only what I have called the intelligent class who really possess this heritage. They of course possess it in varying degrees, but most of them possess enough of it to give them dominion over those who do not possess it.

. . . social heredity is not a process of organic transmission, that no part of the social germ-plasm passes from one individual to another, but that all knowledge must be separately acquired by every individual. The social organization must be such as to infuse it into the members of society as fast as they are capable of receiving it. This infusion of it is social transmission, and unless it is infused it is not transmitted. The only way in which products of past achievement have been preserved has been through such a degree of social organization as is sufficient to infuse them into a certain number of the members of society. This number has always, in the historical races, been large enough to prevent their being lost, and most or all human achievement has been preserved. But it is easy to imagine this great social duty to be neglected and all human achievement lost. There are parts of the world in which this has virtually happened, and this is the way in which races degenerate.

But society has never and nowhere been so organized as to transmit the products of achievement to more than a small fraction of its members. These constitute the intelligent class. The rest are all intellectually disinherited, and while the intellectually disinherited always include and are nearly coextensive with the materially disinherited, the former is much the more serious condition. . . . For the intellectual inheritance would bring with it the material inheritance and all the other advantages that are enjoyed by the intelligent class. Of all the problems of applied sociology that which towers above all others is the problem of the organization of society so that the heritage of the past shall be transmitted to all its members alike. Until this problem is solved there is scarcely any use in trying to solve other problems. Not only are most of them otherwise incapable of solution, but this primary problem once solved all others will solve themselves.

But here we encounter the great sullen, stubborn error, so universal and ingrained as to constitute a world view, that the difference between the upper and lower classes of society is due to a difference in their intellectual capacity, something existing in the nature of things, something preordained and inherently inevitable. Every form of sophistry is employed to uphold this virtue. We are told that there must be social classes, that they are a necessary part of the social order. There must be laborers and unskilled workmen to do the drudgery work of the world. There must be menial servants to wait upon us. . . .

All of which, while clearly showing that the persons who thus argue not only fear but believe that the lower classes are capable of being raised to their own level, reveals a lack of reflection and an incapacity for logical reasoning scarcely to be met with elsewhere. It recalls the remark of the Scotch engineer whom some fortune transported to the plains of Kansas before the days of Pacific railroads, that there could be no railroads in that country, for "where are the hills to put the tunnels through?"

. . . . with . . . qualifications the doctrine of the equal intellectual capacity of all men is a perfectly sound doctrine, and is the doctrine upon which the applied sociologist must stand. It is true that this view has appearances against it, but, as I have often shown, there is no great truth in any department of science that did not at first have appearances against it. The whole march of truth has consisted in substituting the hidden and obscure reality for the falsely apparent. With this uniform trend of history before us, we ought by this time to have learned to suspect everything that seems on the face of it to be true. Let us glance at some of the evidence in favor of the Helvetian doctrine and against the current belief.

Rise of the Proletariat. The history of social classes furnishes to the philosophical student of society the most convincing proof that the lower grades of mankind have never occupied those positions on account of any inherent incapacity to occupy higher ones. Throughout antiquity and well down through the Middle Ages the great mass of mankind were slaves. A little later they were serfs bound to the soil. Finally, with the abolition of slavery, the fall of the feudal system, and the establishment of the industrial system, this great mass took the form of a proletariat, the fourth estate, considered of so little consequence that they are seldom mentioned by the great historians of Europe. Even at the close of the eighteenth century, when the greatest of all political revolutions occurred, it was only the third estate that was at all in evidence—the business class, bourgeoisie, or social mesoderm. This class had been looked down upon and considered inferior, and only the lords spiritual and temporal were regarded as capable of controlling social and national affairs. This class is now at the top. It has furnished the world's brains for two centuries, and if there is any intellectual inferiority it is to be found in the poor remnant that still calls itself the nobility in some countries.

The movement that is now agitating society is different from any of the previous movements, but it differs from them only as they differed from one another. It is nothing less than the coming to consciousness of the proletariat. The class who for ages were slaves or serfs are now voters in enlightened states. They have risen to where they can begin to see out, and they are rising still higher. When a new truth begins to dawn and replace an old error it is always found that the weightiest facts in support of the truth have been furnished by the defenders of the error. The best arguments for organic evolution were supplied by such anti-evolutionists as Baer, Agassiz, and Virchow. Nearly all the facts needed to establish the gynaecocentric theory were drawn from writings specially designed to support the androcentric theory. And now we find one of the strongest believers in the essential distinction between social classes unconsciously arguing for intellectual egalitarianism. Says Mr. Benjamin Kidd:

One of the most striking and significant signs of the times is the spectacle of Demos, with these new battlecries ringing in his ears, gradually emerging from the long silence of social and political serfdom. Not now does he come with the violence of revolution foredoomed to failure, but with the slow and majestic progress which marks a natural evolution. He is no longer unwashed and illiterate, for we have universal education. He is no longer muzzled and without political power, for we have universal suffrage. . . . The advance towards more equal conditions of life has been so great, that amongst the more progressive nations such terms as lower orders, common people, and working classes are losing much of their old meaning, the masses of the people are being slowly raised, and the barriers of birth, class, and privilege are everywhere being broken through. But, on the other hand, the pulses of life have not slackened amongst us; the rivalry is keener, the stress severer, and the pace quicker than ever before. . . . The power-holding classes are in full conscious retreat before the incoming people.[1]

All this is true, though somewhat overdrawn, but Kidd is so blinded by the current world view that he will not attribute it to the slowly growing intelligence of the masses. He attributes it to the rise and spread of humanitarianism, which by an obvious bid for the applause of the religious world he falsely calls religion, and repeats Comte's

[1] Social Evolution, pp. 10, 55, 300.

saying that man is becoming more and more religious.[2] He dimly
perceives the fact that there has been emotional development as well
as brain development, and properly enough emphasizes the truth that
this growth of sympathy on the part of the upper classes has greatly
accelerated the rise of the lower classes. But he attributes it all to
such agencies and strangely confounds the ethical with the religious
and supernatural, virtually arguing that the less rational the people are
the faster they will rise, and ascribing all human progress to the influence of "ultra-rational sanctions," i.e., to superstition. He flatly de-
nies that intelligence has anything to do with the matter, saying:

Another explanation, currently offered, is that the result is caused by
the growing strength and intelligence of the people's party which render
the attack irresistible. But we may readily perceive that the increasing
strength and intelligence of the lower classes of the community is the
result of the change which is in progress, and that it cannot, therefore, be
by itself the cause.[3]

I ought perhaps to apologize for giving so prominent a place to a
book which is so obviously written for applause; but Mr. Kidd has a
really keen insight into social questions and has contributed much
to their elucidation, still, by trimming his sails to catch every breeze,
he has made his book a tissue of inconsistencies. It has had a wide
influence for both good and evil, and it is doing much to prop up
and perpetuate the error we are here combating and to postpone the
acceptance of the truth that is destined ultimately to replace it. But
he has not himself been able to shut his eyes entirely to the native
capacity of the lower classes for education, and in at least one passage
he practically admits their substantial equality with the upper classes
in this respect:

It is not yet clearly perceived by the people that there is not any more
natural and lasting distinction between the *educated* and *uneducated*
classes of which we hear so much nowadays, than there has been between
the other classes in the past. Citizen and slave, patrician and plebeian,
feudal lord and serf, privileged classes and common people, leisured classes
and working masses, have been steps in a process of development.[4]

What has actually taken place in the history of the world has been
a gradual upward movement of the mass from the condition of mere

[2] Testament d'Auguste Comte, Paris, 1884, p. 90.
[3] Social Evolution, p. 176.
[4] Social Evolution, pp. 234–235.

slaves to that of more or less skilled laborers with some general ideas about the land they live in and the world at large, until from a state in which at least nine tenths were submerged there is now in enlightened countries only a completely "submerged tenth." But there nevertheless exists in fact only a completely emerged tenth. The essential fact, however, is that there is no valid reason why not only the other partially emerged eight tenths but the completely submerged tenth should not all completely emerge. They are all equally capable of it. This does not at all imply that all men are equal intellectually. It only insists that intellectual inequality is common to all classes, and is as great among the members of the completely emerged tenth as it is between that class and the completely submerged tenth. Or, to state it more clearly, if the same individuals who constitute the intelligent class at any time or place had been surrounded from their birth by exactly the same conditions that have surrounded the lowest stratum of society, they would have inevitably found themselves in that stratum; and if an equal number taken at random of the lowest stratum of society had been surrounded from their birth by exactly the same conditions . . . by which the intelligent class have been surrounded, they would in fact have constituted the intelligent class instead of the particular individuals who happen actually to constitute it. In other words, class distinctions in society are wholly artificial, depend entirely on environing conditions, and are in no sense due to differences in native capacity. Differences in native capacity exist and are as great as they have ever been pictured, but they exist in all classes alike.